SAFETY

Classroom Safety Tips:

- Read all steps a few times before you start.

- Listen to the teacher.

- When you see this ▨, it means for you to be careful.

- ◥◣ Wear goggles or gloves when told.

- Wear old clothes.

- Be careful with glass and sharp objects.

- Never taste or smell things unless your teacher tells you to.

- Tell about spills right away.

- Report accidents right away.

- Keep your work place neat.

- Clean up when you are done.

Outside Safety Tips:

- Listen to the teacher.

- Stay with your group.

- Never taste or smell things unless your teacher tells you to.

- Don't touch plants or animals unless your teacher tells you to.

- Put living things back where you found them.

- Report accidents right away.

McGRAW-HILL

SCIENCE

MACMILLAN/McGRAW-HILL EDITION

RICHARD MOYER ■ LUCY DANIEL ■ JAY HACKETT

PRENTICE BAPTISTE ■ PAMELA STRYKER ■ JOANNE VASQUEZ

NATIONAL
GEOGRAPHIC
SOCIETY

McGraw-Hill
School Division

New York   Farmington

PROGRAM AUTHORS

Dr. Lucy H. Daniel
*Teacher, Consultant
Rutherford County Schools,
North Carolina*

Dr. Jay Hackett
*Emeritus Professor of Earth
Sciences
University of Northern
Colorado*

Dr. Richard H. Moyer
*Professor of Science
Education
University of Michigan-
Dearborn*

Dr. H. Prentice Baptiste
*Professor of Curriculum and
Instruction
New Mexico State
University*

Pamela Stryker, M.Ed.
*Elementary Educator and
Science Consultant
Eanes Independent School
District
Austin, Texas*

JoAnne Vasquez, M.Ed.
*Elementary Science
Education Specialist
Mesa Public Schools,
Arizona
NSTA President 1996–1997*

NATIONAL
GEOGRAPHIC
SOCIETY

Washington, D.C.

CONTRIBUTING AUTHORS

Dr. Thomas Custer
Dr. James Flood
Dr. Diane Lapp
Doug Llewellyn
Dorothy Reid
Dr. Donald M. Silver

CONSULTANTS

Dr. Danny J. Ballard
Dr. Carol Baskin
Dr. Bonnie Buratti
Dr. Suellen Cabe
Dr. Shawn Carlson
Dr. Thomas A. Davies
Dr. Marie DiBerardino
Dr. R. E. Duhrkopf
Dr. Ed Geary
Dr. Susan C. Giarratano-Russell
Dr. Karen Kwitter
Dr. Donna Lloyd-Kolkin
Ericka Lochner, RN
Donna Harrell Lubcker
Dr. Dennis L. Nelson
Dr. Fred S. Sack
Dr. Martin VanDyke
Dr. E. Peter Volpe
Dr. Josephine Davis Wallace
Dr. Joe Yelderman

McGraw-Hill School Division

A Division of The McGraw·Hill Companies

Copyright © 2000 McGraw-Hill School Division,
a Division of the Educational and Professional
Publishing Group of The McGraw-Hill Companies, Inc.

McGraw-Hill School Division
Two Penn Plaza
New York, New York 10121

Printed in the United States of America

ISBN 0-02-277433-5 / 1

3 4 5 6 7 8 9 004/046 05 04 03 02 01 00 99

CONTENTS

UNIT 1 · A TREE

UNIT 2 THE SKY

UNIT 4 · ON THE MOVE

UNIT 5 A POND

UNIT 6

HUMAN BODY: BEING YOU

REFERENCE SECTION

PICTURE BUILDERS

Life at the Pond

ACTIVITIES

READING PICTURES AND CHARTS

FACTS, PROBLEMS, AND PUZZLES

NATIONAL GEOGRAPHIC
FUNTASTIC FACTS

YOUR TEXTBOOK at a Glance

Begin each topic with an **Explore** question. Then try an **Explore Activity.**

World of SCIENCE
NATIONAL GEOGRAPHIC

Geography Link

Some rain sinks into the ground.

SCIENCE MAGAZINE

History of Science

MOON WALK

In 1969, America sent *Apollo 11* to the Moon.
The spacecraft carried three astronauts.
Two of them walked on the Moon.

The other astronaut stayed in *Apollo 11*.
He flew around the Moon.
Then he flew everyone back to Earth!

Later, other Apollo spacecraft landed on the Moon.
Astronauts took pictures.
They brought back Moon rocks.
We learned a lot about the Moon.

DISCUSS

1. When did the first person walk on the Moon?
2. Why do you think it's hard to get to the Moon?

Topic 6
PHYSICAL SCIENCE

Why it matters

Heat can change ...d's and liquids.

...nce Word

...ange from a ... a liquid

Matter Can Change

Look at the snowman.
What is it made of?
Is it a solid?
How can you tell?

EXPLORE

What will happen to the snowman?

Read the **Science Magazines. National Geographic World of Science** is the first magazine in each unit.

Brain Power

Why would the tall grasses

NATIONAL GEOGRAPHIC

FUNtastic Facts

The blue whale is huge.
It is the biggest animal.
It has the mass of 30 elephants!
What else has that much mass?

Answer fun questions about real-world facts.

EXPLORE ✹ ACTIVITY

Can a solid change to a liquid?

Ice is a solid. What happens to ice in a warm place?

What you need
- ice cube
- cup
- *Science Journal*

What to do

1. Write your name on the cup.
2. Place the ice cube in the cup.
3. Place the cup in a sunny or a warm place.
4. **Observe** Wait 15 minutes. See what happens to the ice cube.
5. **Record** Write what happens in the *Science Journal*.

What did you find out?

1. What happened to the ice cube?
2. **Infer** Can a solid change to a liquid?

UNIT REVIEW

PROBLEMS and PUZZLES

The Shadow Knows

When is the Sun's shadow longest?
Place a stick in the ground.
Trace its shadow in the morning.
Trace its shadow at noon.
Trace its shadow in the afternoon.

Make a Constellation

Make a constellation model.
Trace the pattern on a card.
Poke the holes in the card.
Darken the room.
Shine a flashlight on the pattern.

UNIT REVIEW

Use Science Words

| gases | matter | measure | melt | properties |

1. You find out how big a thing is when you __?__.
2. Fuzzy, small, and black are __?__ of some kittens.
3. Everything is made of __?__.
4. Balloons are filled with __?__.
5. Heat can make ice __?__.

Use Science Ideas

6. Is a penny a solid, a liquid, or a gas?
7. How can you tell that air is real?
8. Which has more matter, a bike or a bus?
9. What are some different liquids?
10. **Measure** How wide is this page? Use paper clips.

Write in Your Journal
What do you see? Write about it.

▲ Have fun solving **Problems and Puzzles.** Write in the *Science Journal* about what you learn.

▲ Build your skills with **Skill Builders.** Use the **Handbook** for help.

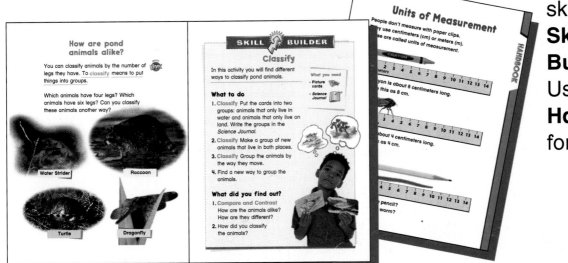

How are pond animals alike?

You can classify animals by the number of legs they have. To classify means to put things into groups.

Which animals have four legs? Which animals have six legs? Can you classify these animals another way?

Water Strider
Raccoon
Turtle
Dragonfly

SKILL BUILDER

Classify

In this activity you will find different ways to classify pond animals.

What you need
- Picture cards
- Science Journal

What to do

1. **Classify** Put the cards into two groups: animals that only live in water and animals that only live on land. Write the groups in the *Science Journal*.
2. **Classify** Make a group of new animals that live in both places.
3. **Classify** Group the animals by the way they move.
4. Find a new way to group the animals.

What did you find out?

1. **Compare and Contrast** How are the animals alike? How are they different?
2. How did you classify the animals?

Units of Measurement

People don't measure with paper clips. They use centimeters (cm) or meters (m). These are called units of measurement.

...yon is about 8 centimeters long. ...e this as 8 cm.

...bout 4 centimeters long. ...as 4 cm.

...pencil? ...worm?

HANDBOOK

INVITATION TO SCIENCE

Christina Allen

This scientist has her
own tree house!
She sits quietly and watches
animals come and go.
Her name is Christina Allen.
She studies animals that
live in the rain forest.

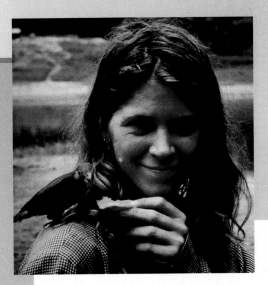

Christina likes animals! When she was a child, she cared for stray animals. Her parents let her keep some.

Many trees in the rain forest have been cut down. Animals need trees for homes and for food. Christina wants to learn all she can about animals and rain forests. Then she can tell people why rain forests should be saved.

Squirrel monkeys live in the rain forest.

Christina studies a giant snail.

BE A SCIENTIST

Your doctor helps you when you are sick. Your doctor helps you stay healthy. How is your doctor like a scientist?

EXPLORE

Why does a doctor ask questions?

What can you learn about your body?

In this activity you'll measure different parts of your body.

What you need

- **measuring tape**
- *Science Journal*

What to do

1. Work with a partner.

2. **Measure** Use measuring tape to measure how tall you are. Write the number in the *Science Journal*.

3. **Measure** Stretch out your arms. Use measuring tape to measure how long your arms are.

What did you find out?

1. Who is taller, you or your partner? Who has longer arms?

2. Which is longer, your height or your arms?

3. What could a doctor learn by measuring you?

How do scientists work?

The Explore Activity shows one way
a doctor works.
The doctor measures parts of you.
She measures how tall you are.
She measures how much you weigh.
She measures your temperature.
Sometimes this can tell the doctor
that you are sick.

A doctor is a scientist who helps
people stay healthy.
Dr. Denege Ward works in Michigan.
Her job is to help people get better.

Dr. Ward visits her patients in
the hospital.
She asks them questions.
She writes down notes.

Dr. Ward also sees patients in
her office.
Some patients are babies.
Some patients are older people.
Sometimes she goes to patients who
cannot come to her.

What questions might a doctor ask
a patient?
In what ways might a doctor help a
patient during a visit?

How do scientists work with each other?

If you aren't sure of something, what do you do?
You might ask other people to help.

What do you think doctors do?
When doctors need to find out something, they ask other doctors.
Sometimes doctors read books to find answers.

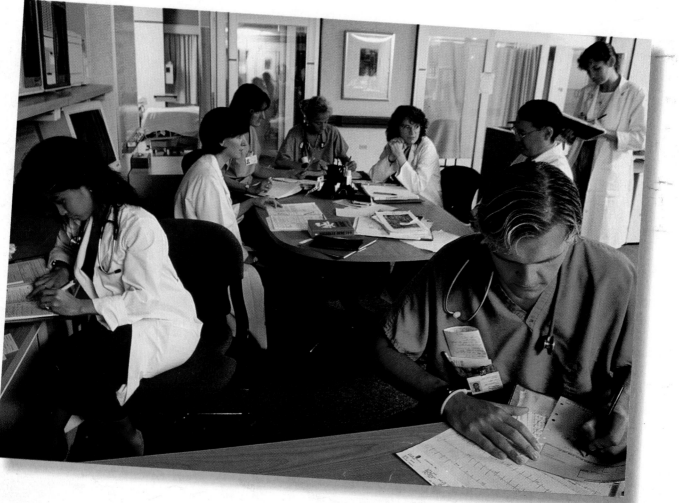

Doctors use a computer.
They can write about patients on the computer.
Doctors can use a computer to find out what makes people sick.
Computers can help doctors take care of their patients.

How do scientists test things?

Doctors help sick people in many ways.

They talk to them to find out how they are sick.

Sometimes they test a patient's body to learn more.

Doctors use many tools to do these tests.

Another tool takes pictures of your bones.

The tests help doctors understand how to help a patient.
A patient might need medicine to get better.
Sometimes a patient might have to stay in a hospital.

How can I be like a scientist?

Scientists start with questions.
They look at things around them.

A doctor looks at a sick person
and asks questions.
Doctors use tools to find answers.

Have you ever asked questions
about something?
Being a scientist means looking for
answers to questions!

In the Explore Activity, a question
was asked.
You made a plan to find an answer.
You used measuring tape to measure
parts of your body.
You found out which was longer.
You wrote your answer in the
Science Journal.
You did it like a scientist!

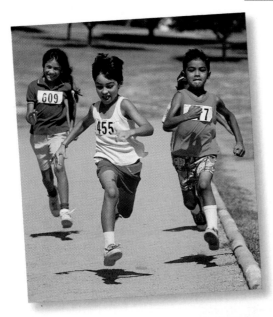

Doctors help us stay healthy.
When we're healthy, we can do all
the things we need to do.
We can be with our family.
We can play with our friends.
We can go to school.
We can be a scientist!

S16

REVIEW

1. What does a doctor do to find out why people are sick?

2. What tools does a doctor use to find out why people are sick?

3. How does a doctor learn more about helping people?

BE A SCIENTIST Glossary

A

ask to make up a question you want to find the answer to

C

cause and effect how one thing changes another thing

classify to put things into groups

communicate to talk, write or draw

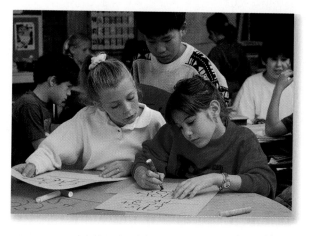

compare and contrast to look at things to see how they are the same and how they are different

conclude to make a decision based on all the things you know

D

decide to choose from different ideas or things

E

explain to help somebody understand something

G

get information to find out facts about something

I

identify to know something by name

infer to use what you know to figure something out

M

measure — to find out the size or amount of something

O

observe to use your senses to learn something

P

plan to choose how you are going to do something

predict to guess what is going to happen in the future

put in order to place things in a way that's easy to use

U

use numbers to show how much there is of something

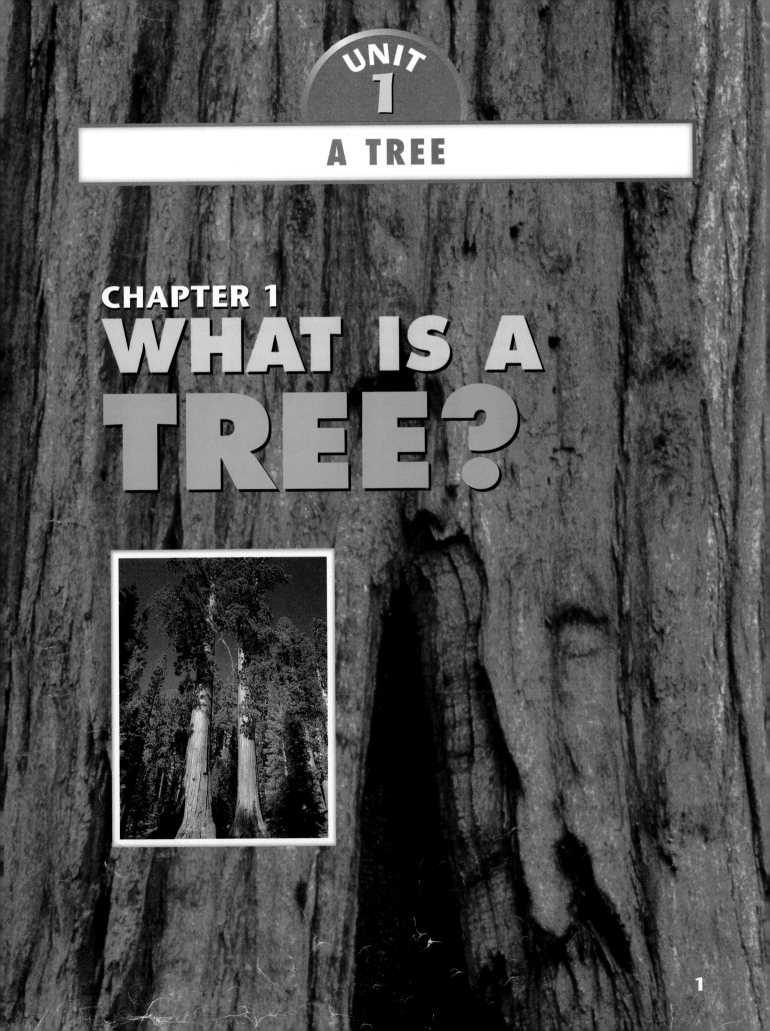

CHAPTER 1

WHAT IS A TREE?

Topic
LIFE SCIENCE
1

Why it matters

A tree has many parts.

Science Words

leaves the part that makes food for a tree

roots the part that takes in water for a tree

observe use your senses to learn something

trunk the part that is the stem of a tree

branches the part that holds the leaves of a tree

The Parts of a Tree

Are there trees where you live?
Do they look like these trees?
How do they look the same?
How do they look different?

EXPLORE

Have you ever looked closely at a leaf?
Do all leaves look alike?

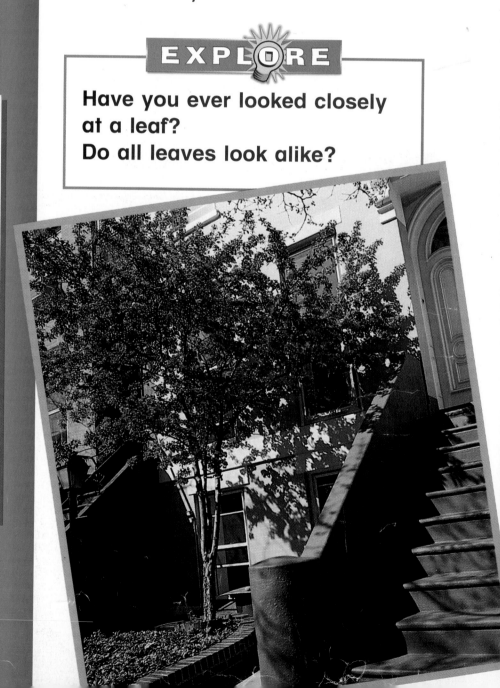

How are leaves different?

Let's look at different leaves.

What you need

- 2 different leaves
- crayon
- paper
- *Science Journal*

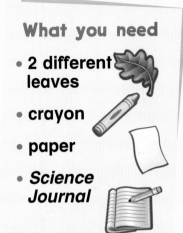

What to do

1. Place the paper on a leaf.

2. Rub the crayon over the paper.

3. Use a different leaf.
   Do steps 1 and 2 again.

What did you find out?

1. Write about the edges of each leaf in the *Science Journal.*

2. **Compare** Tell about the lines that run through each leaf.

What are the parts of a tree?

Are there trees where you live?
A tree is a plant.
It has many parts.

The Explore Activity shows that
leaves can be different.
The leaves are one part
of a tree.
Leaves make food
for a tree.

Oak Tree

leaves

Roots are another part of a tree.
Roots take in water.
Roots grow under the ground.
Roots hold a tree in place.

NATIONAL GEOGRAPHIC

FUNtastic Facts

Roots can grow very deep.
They grow long.
Why do they grow long?

roots

How can you tell these plants apart?

How are these plants alike?
How are they different?
What parts do you see?
You can observe plants.
When you observe, you look, touch, taste,
hear, or smell to learn about something.

Observe

In this activity you will observe different parts of a plant.

What you need
- a plant
- hand lens
- *Science Journal*

What to do

1. **Observe** Look at the parts of the plant with a hand lens.

2. **Observe** Touch the parts of the plant.

   ▨ SAFETY: Do not taste the plant.

3. **Observe** Smell the parts of the plant.

4. Draw what you observe in the *Science Journal*.

   ▨ SAFETY: Wash your hands.

What did you find out?

1. Which senses did you use to observe the plant?

2. Tell about the parts of the plant you observed.

What are other parts of a tree?

Another part of a tree is the trunk.
The trunk is the stem of a tree.
It holds up the tree.

Big branches grow out of the trunk.
The branches hold the leaves.

branches

trunk

Oak Tree

A plane needs all
its parts to fly.
A tree also needs its parts.
All the parts work together.
They help a tree to live.

REVIEW

1. What part of a tree makes food?

2. What part of a tree takes in water?

3. What holds up the leaves on a tree?

4. **Observe** How many senses could you use to observe a real tree?

5. **Think and Write** Draw a tree. Label its parts.

9

Why it matters

Trees need water, sunlight, and room to grow.

Science Word

living thing grows and changes

The Needs of Trees

What do you need to live and grow?
Could you live and grow without water?

EXPLORE

Why do you think plants need water?

What happens to a plant that does not get water?

In this activity you can observe what happens to a plant that is not watered.

What you need

- 2 plants marked: *water* and *no water*
- hand lens
- *Science Journal*

What to do

1. **Observe** Look at the plant marked *water*. Use the hand lens.

2. Draw what you observe in the *Science Journal*. List words to describe what you see.

3. Do steps 1 and 2 for the plant marked *no water*.

What did you find out?

1. What did each plant look like?

2. What happens when a plant does not get water?

no water

water

What do trees need?

Trees are living things.
Living things grow and change.
A living thing needs water and food.
The Explore Activity shows that a plant
dries up without water.

Where do trees get water?
When it rains, water sinks into the soil.
The roots take in the water.

Trees need sunlight, too.
Leaves use sunlight to make food.
Food from its leaves helps a tree grow.

A tree cannot live without food and water.

juniper tree

mangrove tree

What else do trees need?

Some trees do not have enough room.
Roots need room to spread out.
Leaves need room to get sunlight.

A plane needs gas to fly.
A tree needs sunlight,
water, and room to grow.
A tree cannot live without them.
Which tree might not grow tall?
Why?

REVIEW

1. Are trees living things? Why or why not.

2. What do roots take into the tree?

3. What do leaves help make for the tree?

4. **Observe** What part is missing from this tree?

5. **Think and Write** It has not rained all spring. What may happen to the trees?

Why it matters

Trees can grow from seeds.

Science Words

seed has a young plant inside

seedling a small new plant

Trees Grow

Did you know that apples grow on trees?
Some apples are sweet to eat.
Did you ever bite into an apple?
What was inside?

EXPLORE

Were there seeds in the apple? Do all apples have the same number of seeds?

How many seeds are inside an apple?

MATH LINK

Do this activity to find out.

What to do

SAFETY: Let your teacher cut the apple.

1. **Predict** How many seeds are in an apple? Write your guess in the *Science Journal*.

2. Take out all of the seeds.

3. **Use Numbers** Count the seeds. Write the number.

What did you find out?

1. How many seeds did you find? Was your guess close?

2. **Compare** Talk with 2 friends. Did all the apples have the same number of seeds?

What you need

- apple
- paper towel
- plastic knife
- *Science Journal*

How do trees grow?

The Explore Activity shows that apples do not have the same number of seeds. Apple trees grow from apple seeds. The seed has the young plant inside. The seed is planted in the ground.

Soon the seed becomes a seedling. A seedling is a small, new plant.

1 seeds

2 seedling

The seedling grows into a young tree.

After a few years, the tree grows apples.
Its seeds can be used to grow many
more apple trees.

③ tree

④ apple with
seeds

How are seeds different?

Seeds come in all shapes and sizes.
A seed grows into its own kind of plant.
Maple seeds grow into maple trees.

Which kind of trees will grow from these seeds?

seeds from a chestnut tree

seeds from an oak tree

seeds
from a
maple
tree

20

Seeds are very important. If there were no seeds, there would be no trees. If there were no trees, there would be no apples, nuts, or other foods that grow on trees.

REVIEW

1. What do trees grow from?

2. What is a small, new plant called?

3. How are seeds different?

4. **Observe** Which tree is a seedling? How do you know?

A   B

5. **Think and Write** Draw an apple.

Topic
LIFE SCIENCE
4

Why it matters

Trees change in many ways all year.

Science Word

evergreen stays green all year

Trees Change

Do you think these pictures show the same tree?
Tell why.
What is different about them?

EXPLORE

**Do you know how trees change?
Tell about these changes.**

How do trees change?

We can observe these changes and tell about them.

What you need

- **Picture Cards**
- *Science Journal*

What to do

1. **Observe** Look at the pictures of the tree. How has it changed?

2. Place the pictures in order. Start with spring.

3. Write the order in the *Science Journal*.

What did you find out?

How can trees change?

23

How do trees change?

The Explore Activity shows that trees change.
Trees change all year long.
An apple tree changes in many ways.

Flowers grow on the apple tree in spring.
Leaves begin to grow.

Apples grow on the tree in summer.

spring

summer

24

The apples are picked in the fall.
The leaves turn yellow and brown.
Then they fall off the tree.

The tree has no leaves or apples in winter.

Soon spring will come again.
What will happen to the tree in spring?

fall

winter

How do other trees change?

This tree is an evergreen.
An evergreen stays green all year.
The leaves of evergreen trees
are called needles.
Most evergreen trees do not lose
all of their needles in the fall.
New needles grow in the spring.

Brain Power

How did evergreens get
their name?

You have changed as you have grown.
Trees change, too.
Trees would not grow new leaves and fruits
if they did not change.

REVIEW

1. How do trees change during the year?

2. When is the best time to pick apples?

3. What kind of trees stay green all winter?

4. **Observe** Look at the fruits on this page. How are they different?

5. **ART LINK Think and Write** Draw an apple tree in spring, summer, fall, and winter.

Counting Rings

A tree may
grow for years.
Sometimes a tree dies.
It has to be cut down.

Here is a piece from a
tree that was cut down.
Can you see the rings?
A tree grows a ring each year.

A Closer Look

Why are some rings wide
and some rings thin?
Sun and rain help a tree grow.

Some years there's lots of
sun and rain.
The tree grows wide rings.

Some years it hardly rains. The
tree grows thin rings.

Discuss

1 What can we learn from tree rings?

2 Look at the piece of tree.
Was the tree older than you?

Use Science Words

branches
evergreen
leaves
observe
roots
seed
seedling
trunk

1. The tree takes in sunlight to make food through the ___?___. page 4

2. When you touch, look at, taste or smell something, you ___?___ it. page 6

3. The tree is held in the ground by the ___?___. page 5

4. The tree is held up by the ___?___. page 8

5. The leaves are held up by the ___?___. page 8

6. A young plant is inside a ___?___. page 18

7. A small, new plant is a ___?___. page 18

8. A tree that stays green all winter is an ___?___. page 26

Use Science Ideas

9. Name the four parts of a tree. pages 4–5, 8

10. **Observe** What does this tree need? page 10

PROBLEMS and PUZZLES

Leaf Hunt Go outside. Collect different leaves. Do any of them look alike? How can you sort the leaves?

CHAPTER 2
HOW WE USE TREES

Why it matters

Many things we use every day come from trees.

Science Word

natural resource
something we use that comes from Earth

People Need Trees

What would life be like without any trees?

Many things are made from trees. Even paper is made from trees. The book you are reading was made from a tree!

EXPLORE

Look closely at this picture. How many things can you find that are made from trees?

How do we use trees every day?

Let's find things that come from trees.

What to do

1. **Observe** Find pictures of things made from wood. Cut these pictures out.

   ▨ **SAFETY:** Be careful with scissors.

2. Glue them on the paper.

3. Write how we use trees in the *Science Journal*.

What did you find out?

1. Make a list of things made from trees.

2. How many things did you find?

What you need

- magazines
- scissors
- large piece of paper
- glue
- *Science Journal*

What comes from trees?

The Explore Activity shows that
many things come from trees.
All these things came from trees.

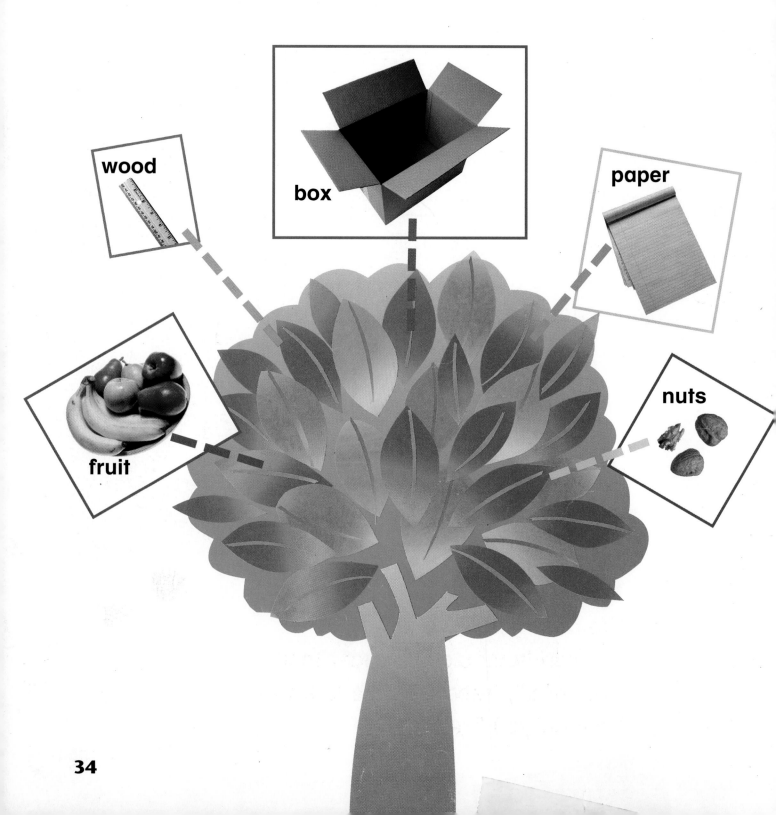

wood

box

paper

fruit

nuts

Trees give us other things, too.
They give us shade on a hot day.
We can rest under them.
We can have picnics under them.
Best of all, trees are nice to look at.
Why do you like trees?

Could we run out of trees?

We cut trees down to use.

Trees are a **natural resource**.

A natural resource is something we use that comes from Earth.

To make sure we don't run out of trees, people plant more.

What would you miss if there were no trees?
Would you miss the shade?
Would you miss the fruits and nuts?
Trees are a big part of your life.

REVIEW

1. List two things that we get from trees.

2. What is a natural resource?

3. Why do people plant more trees?

4. **Observe** Which item comes from trees?

5. **Think and Write** How do you enjoy trees?

Why it matters

Many animals live in trees.

Science Word

shelter something that covers or protects

Animals Need Trees

Do you know where birds sleep?
Many birds sleep in trees.
They build their homes in trees.
These homes are called nests.

EXPLORE

How did this bird make its nest?

How do birds use trees?

Can birds use leaves for nests?

What to do

1. Cut out the paper leaf.

   ▨ **SAFETY:** Be careful with scissors.

2. Your teacher will poke 4 holes on each side of the leaf.

3. Thread the yarn through the holes. Pull the yarn tight.

4. Tape the yarn to the leaf.

5. Add grass inside the nest.

6. **Predict** Guess how many stones your nest can hold. Write the number in the *Science Journal*.

7. One by one, add stones.

What did you find out?

1. How many stones could your nest hold?

2. Why does this bird need a tree?

What you need

- paper leaf
- yarn
- tape
- scissors
- grass
- stones
- *Science Journal*

39

Why do animals need trees?

What animals have you seen in trees?
Animals use trees for shelter.
A shelter covers or protects.
Many animals make their homes in trees.
The Explore Activity
shows that even a leaf
can give shelter.

deer

eagle with young

opossum

Animals get food from trees.
Some animals eat leaves.
Some animals eat seeds.
Other animals eat bugs that
live in trees.

giraffe

raccoon

woodpecker

How do animals help trees?

Animals carry seeds to new places.
Sometimes the seeds fall to the ground.
They may grow into new plants.

Brain Power

How do these animals
help trees?

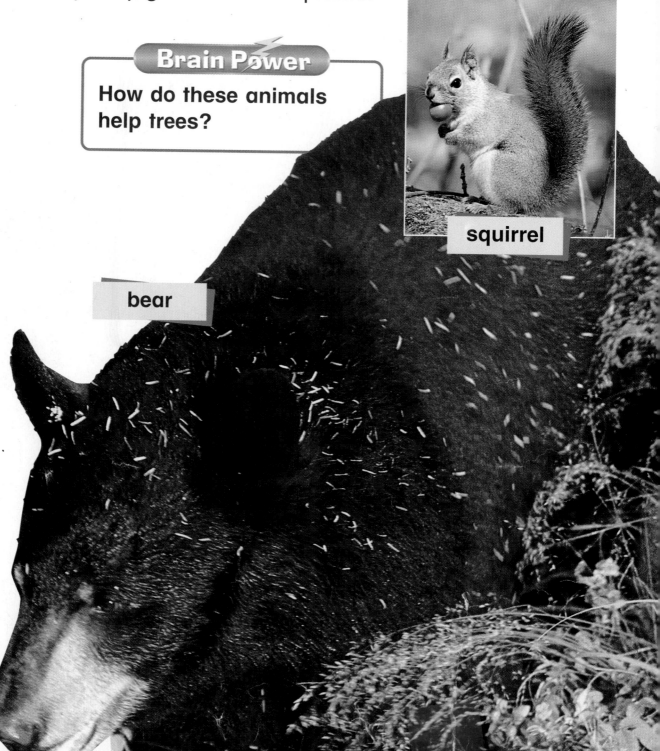

squirrel

bear

Why it matters

Trees matter to many animals.
Some live or hide in trees.
Birds build nests on branches.
Animals get food from trees, too.
How can you help animals that
live in trees?

REVIEW

1. How do trees give animals shelter?

2. What foods do animals get from trees?

3. How do seeds get to new places?

4. **Observe** Why is the bird in the tree?

5. **Think and Write** Draw a tree and an animal that lives in it.

Keeping Trees Healthy

Are there really doctors for trees?

Yes, Jose is a tree doctor.

He cuts off broken branches.

He cuts off wobbly branches, too.

Jose's boots help him climb trees.

The boots have claws like a cat.

Jose uses a chain saw.

It makes a lot of noise!

Jose helps trees in many ways.

He feeds trees that need food.

He cuts back branches so trees get enough sunlight.

Jose cut branches from the apple tree below.

The branches that are left get more light and air.

Now the apples will grow bigger!

DISCUSS

1. How does cutting back tree branches help a tree grow better?

2. What tools does Jose use?

Use Science Words

natural resource
shelter

Match.

1. Something we use that comes from Earth is a ___?___. page 36

2. Animals use trees for ___?___. page 40

Use Science Ideas

3. Which did not come from trees? pages 34–35

   a.   b.   c.   d.

4. Why do birds need trees? pages 40-41

5. Why do giraffes need trees? page 41

6. Why do raccoons need trees? page 41

7. Why do woodpeckers need trees? page 41

8. Why should we try to save trees? page 36

9. Make a list of the ways animals use trees. pages 40-41

10. **Observe** How does this animal help trees? page 42

PROBLEMS and PUZZLES

I Spy a Tree Observe a tree near your home. Observe a leaf and a piece of bark from the tree. Draw a picture of it.

Use Science Words

| evergreen | observe | roots | seedling | shelter |

1. A tree can give a squirrel __?__.

2. A tree is held in the ground by __?__.

3. You can learn about a plant if you __?__ it.

4. A small, new plant is a __?__.

5. An __?__ tree is green all year long.

Use Science Ideas

6. What do roots get from the ground?

7. Name four things made from trees.

8. What can grow from a seed?

9. What does a tree trunk do?

10. **Observe** Is there a tree near your home? Tell about what you have seen in that tree.

Write in Your Journal

What do you see here? Write about it.

PROBLEMS and PUZZLES

The Birthday Tree

Look at these pictures of the Birthday Tree.
Think of a month for each birthday.
Why did you pick that month?

HAPPY BIRTHDAY JAN

HAPPY BIRTHDAY DAN

HAPPY BIRTHDAY STAN

HAPPY BIRTHDAY FRAN

Tree Frame

How do trees help
people and animals?
Make a Tree Frame.
Make branches that say
SHADE, FOOD, WOOD
and SHELTER.
On each leaf, write how
the tree helps.
Make as many leaves as you can.

wood

food

shelter

shade

UNIT 2
THE SKY

CHAPTER 3
THE SKIES ABOVE

Why it matters

The Sun is important for all living things.

Science Words

temperature how warm or cool something is

heat to make warmer or hotter

infer to use what you know to figure something out

The Sun

Do you like to play in the sunshine or in the shade? Look closely at this picture. What are the children wearing? Why do you think this is?

EXPLORE

Is it warmer in the sunshine or in the shade?
How can you find out?

How hot is it?

Measure the temperature in different places.

What you need

- **2 thermometers**
- *Science Journal*

What to do

1. Work with a partner. Pick a sunny place and a shady place.

2. Place your thermometers in those areas. Draw these places in the *Science Journal*.

3. Read the temperature. Is it cold? Warm? Record the temperature.

4. Pick two different places that might be cooler. Repeat steps 2 and 3.

What did you find out?

1. **Compare** Where was it warmer? Where was it cooler?

2. **Conclude** What made the temperature in each place different?

What does the Sun do?

The Explore Activity shows that the temperature can be different.
Temperature tells how warm or cool something is.
The temperature is warmer in the Sun.
It is cooler in the shade.

The temperature can get warmer as the day goes by.
On most days it is warmer in the afternoon than in the morning.

The Sun is very hot.
It lights and **heats** Earth.
To heat means to make warmer or hotter.

It is a hot day!
The Sun heats the sand.
It heats the water and air, too.

Which is warmer?

Look at these two pictures.
Which place is warmer?
How can you tell?

You can **infer** which place
is warmer.
To infer means to use what you know to
figure something out.

Infer from what you observe

In this activity you will use clues to infer which place is warmer.

What you need

- Picture cards
- *Science Journal*

What to do

1. Place the cards with the pictures face up.

2. **Infer** Match 2 cards that show the same season.

What did you find out?

1. **Infer** Which cards were easy to match?

2. What clues helped you decide?

Where is the Sun?

Where is the Sun in the morning?
Where is the Sun in the afternoon?
Where will the Sun be tomorrow morning?
Tomorrow afternoon?
What pattern do you see?

morning

afternoon

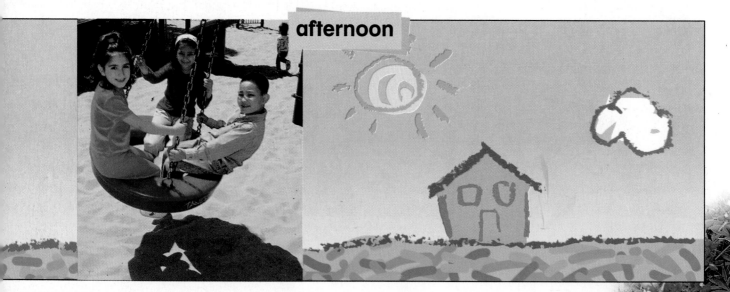

Why it matters

The Sun lights and heats Earth.
Plants need light to make food.
Plants and animals need heat to stay alive.
All living things need the Sun.

REVIEW

1. What does temperature measure?

2. What does the Sun give us?

3. What pattern does the Sun follow?

4. **Infer** It is dark outside. Is it day or night?

5. **Think and Write** Draw a picture of a warm day.

Why it matters

Shadows make shade.

Science Words

shadow made when something is in the way of light

Shadows

Have you ever played a game like this one?
Try to guess what picture the shadows make.
How did you know?

How did the child make those shapes?
Can you make shapes like this?

How can you make shadow shapes?

Do this activity to find out!

What you need

- shadow catcher
- *Science Journal*

What to do

1. Go outside and make a shadow. How can you make the shadow bigger? How can you make the shadow smaller?

2. Find and explore 2 more shadows.

3. Trace the shadows with a partner on the shadow catcher.

4. **Observe** Share your shadow drawings. Can you guess what made each shadow?

What did you find out?

1. **Decide** How did you make a shadow?

2. How did you change the shadows?

What is a shadow?

The Sun is behind the children.
Find the **shadow**.
A shadow is made when something is in
the way of light.
What is blocking the light?

Morning   Afternoon

The Explore Activity shows that
shadows change.
Shadows also change as the Sun
seems to move across the sky.
Find the shadows in the pictures.
How do the shadows change?

Do you always see a shadow?

Sometimes a shadow cannot be seen.
There is not enough sunlight.
Why are there no shadows in this picture?

NATIONAL GEOGRAPHIC

FUNtastic Facts

A sundial tells time.
The shadow moves all day.
Why does the shadow move?
Is there always a shadow?

Have you ever sat in the shade?
Shadows make shade.
They help you stay cool on a very hot day.

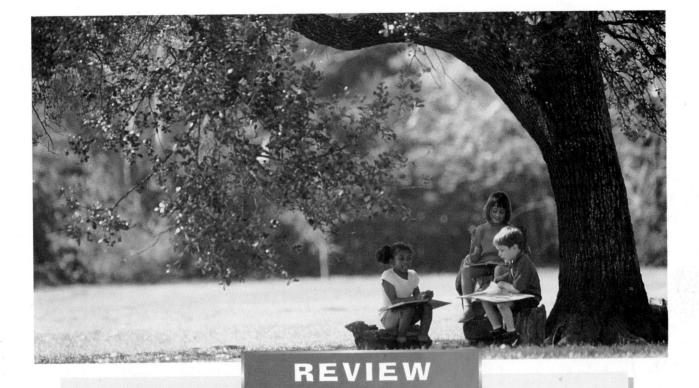

REVIEW

1. How is a shadow made?

2. What happens to shadows between the morning and the afternoon?

3. Why don't you see shadows on a cloudy day?

4. **Infer** What object made this shadow?

5. **Think and Write** Draw a picture of a house and show where the Sun is. Add shadows.

Topic 3
EARTH SCIENCE

Why it matters

Knowing about the weather helps you know what to wear.

Science Words

clouds small drops of water that float in the sky

Weather

What is the weather like in this picture?
Is the weather the same every day?

EXPLORE

In what ways does the weather change?
How can you find out?

What is the weather like?

In this activity you will observe the weather for a week.

What you need
- Weather chart
- thermometer
- *Science Journal*

What to do

1. **Observe** Look at the sky. Is it blue or gray? Record what you see in the *Science Journal*.

2. Measure and record the temperature.

3. Is it cloudy, or raining, or snowing? Record what you observe.

4. Watch the weather for one week. Record in the Weather chart.

What did you find out?

1. What are some changes you observed in the weather?

2. **Compare** Which day was the warmest?

Weather Chart
One week in September

	Monday	Tuesday	Wednesday	Thursday	Friday
It is ☀		✓	✓		
It is ☁				✓	
It is 🌧	✓				
It is ❄					
The temperature is	65°	70°	69°	66	

What is the weather like?

The Explore Activity shows that the weather changes.

The weather can change at any time.
It might be sunny.
Then you see clouds.
The temperature drops.
The wind picks up.
Soon it is raining.

sunny

windy

rainy

Clouds are made from small drops of water that float in the sky.

It rains when clouds become full of big water drops.

What kind of clouds do you see?

fair weather clouds

storm clouds

What are other kinds of weather?

There are other kinds of weather, too.
Tell about the weather in each picture.

snow

hail

fog

Why do you need to know about
the weather?
You need to know what to wear when
you are outside.
You need to know when to go inside
because a storm is coming.

REVIEW

1. What are some kinds of weather?

2. How can weather change?

3. What are clouds made of?

4. **Infer** You look at the sky and think it will rain. What does the sky look like?

5. **ART LINK** **Think and Write** Draw what you would wear when it snows.

Why it matters

The weather changes with the seasons.

Science Words

seasons spring, summer, fall, and winter

Weather and Seasons

What time of year do you like most?
What is the weather like then?
Look at this picture.
The weather is changing.
It is time to take out the warm clothes.

EXPLORE

Can you guess how the weather has changed?

How does weather change over a year?

Lets learn about the weather in different seasons.

What you need

- **Picture Cards**
- *Science Journal*

What to do

1. **Observe** Look at the cards.

2. Group them by seasons.

3. Use words to tell about each group. Write them in the *Science Journal*.

What did you find out?

1. What pictures did you group together that show what could happen on cold days?

2. Draw a picture of something else that would fit in each group.

How does weather change with the seasons?

A year has four **seasons** — spring, summer, fall, and winter.

Summers are hotter. Winters are colder.

Summer

Spring

Fall

Winter

The Explore Activity shows how weather changes from one season to the next.

Which season do you like best?

What is the weather like in other places?

It is summer.
Yet the weather is not the same everywhere.
The weather is different in different places.

In San Antonio, Texas, it is hot and dry.
In San Francisco, California, it is cooler and wetter.

What is summer like where you live?

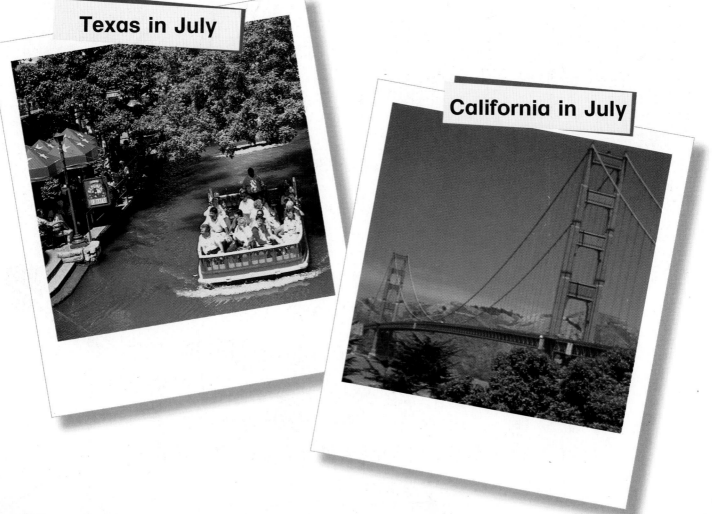

Texas in July

California in July

Seasons are different from place to place.
In winter, it is too cold to grow food in many places.
In most of Florida, it is warm enough to grow food.
That's why you can eat oranges in winter.

REVIEW

1. What are the seasons?

2. How does the weather change from one season to the next?

3. How is the weather in San Antonio different from San Francisco?

4. **Infer** The leaves are falling off the trees. Which season is it? How do you know?

5. **Think and Write** Draw what your school looks like for each of the four seasons.

A Long Winter's Nap

Grizzly bears eat fish, berries, and plants. The bears eat a lot in the summer and fall. They get very fat!

Grizzlies live where there's
lots of ice and snow in winter.
It's hard for the bears to find food.
They find a safe den and take a
long nap.

In spring, the bears wake up.
They are very hungry!

Discuss

1 Why is it hard for grizzly bears to find food in the winter?

2 What do grizzly bears do in the winter?

Use Science Words

clouds
heat
infer
season
shadow
temperature

Match each word to the correct sentence.

1. You can tell how warm or cool a place is by the ___?___. page 52

2. To make warmer or hotter is to ___?___. page 53

3. When you use what you know to figure something out you ___?___. page 54

4. Winter is a ___?___ . page 72

5. When something blocks light it makes a ___?___. page 60

6. Small drops of water that float in the sky are ___?___. page 67

Use Science Ideas

What kinds of weather do you see? pages 66–68

7.   8.   9.

10. **Infer**
    Where is the Sun?
    page 60

PROBLEMS and PUZZLES

Sun Shifts What is the weather like in the summer? Draw a picture.

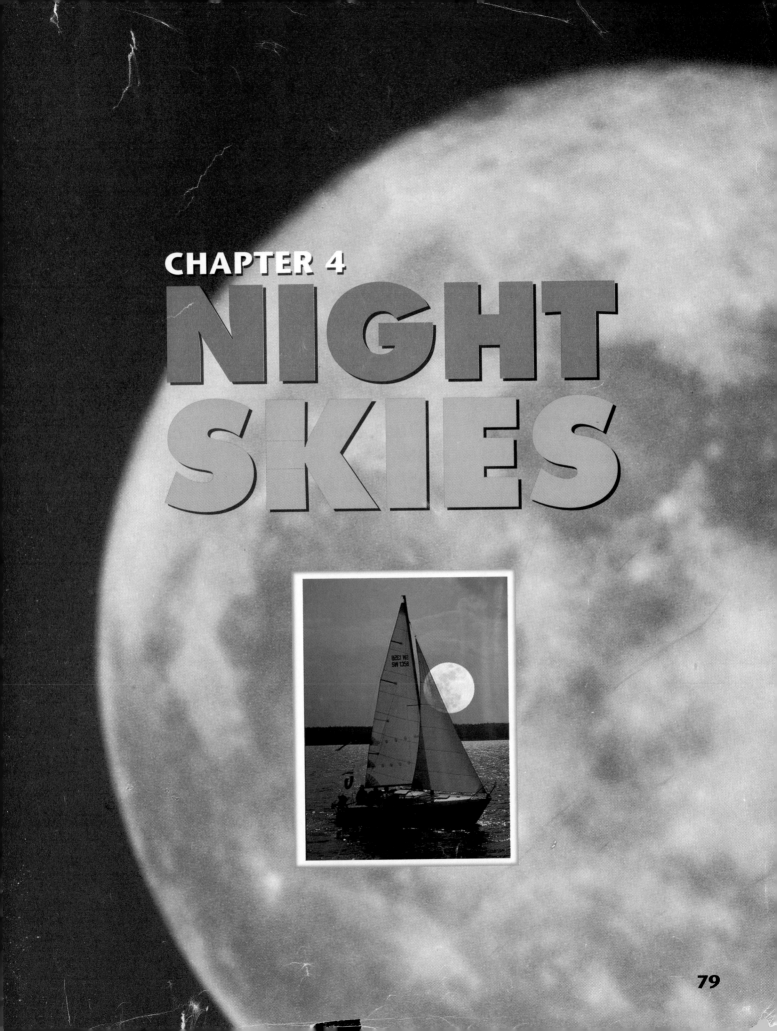

CHAPTER 4
NIGHT SKIES

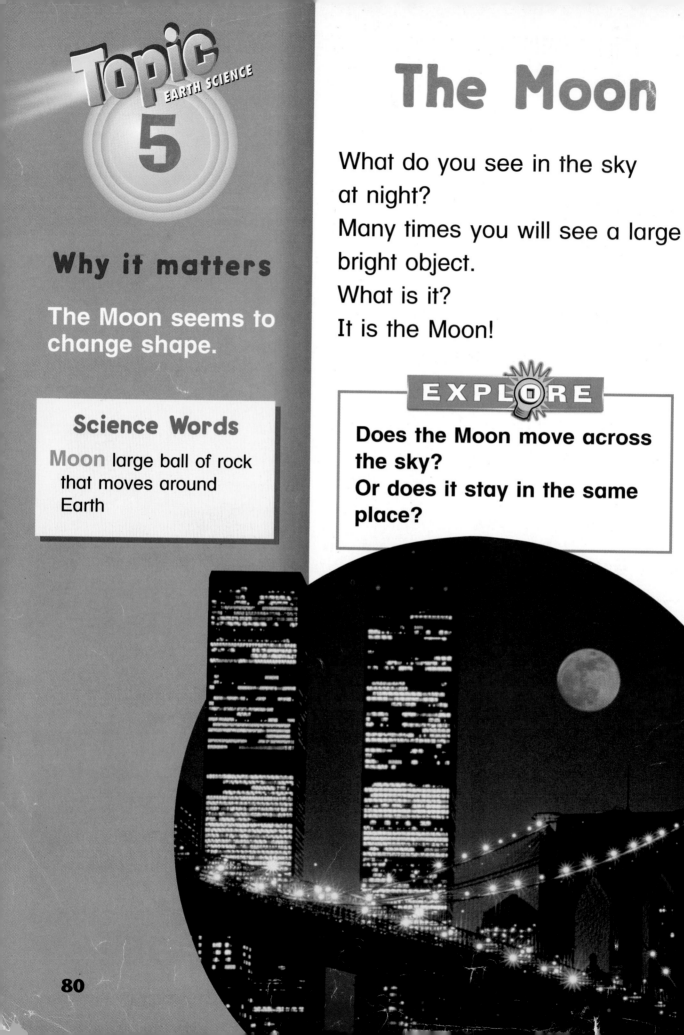

Why it matters

The Moon seems to change shape.

Science Words

Moon large ball of rock that moves around Earth

The Moon

What do you see in the sky at night?
Many times you will see a large bright object.
What is it?
It is the Moon!

EXPLORE

Does the Moon move across the sky?
Or does it stay in the same place?

80

Where is the Moon?

Does the Moon move?
Do this activity to find out.

What you need

- Picture Cards
- *Science Journal*

What to do

1. **Observe** Look at the pictures of the Moon. Can you find the picture that was taken first?

2. Place the pictures in order. Record the order in the *Science Journal.*

3. Where do you think the Moon will be next? Draw a picture.

What did you find out?

1. Does the Moon move?

2. **Explain** Tell how the Moon moves.

How does the Moon change?

The Moon looks big in the night sky.
It is a large ball of rock that moves
around Earth.
The Explore Activity shows that the Moon
moves across the sky.
The Moon changes in other ways, too.
Over time the Moon seems
to change shape.

Crescent Moon

First Quarter Moon

First you do not see any Moon in the sky.
Each night you see more of the Moon.
After about 2 weeks it is round and full.
Then you start to see less of the Moon.
After about 2 more weeks, you only see
a small part.
Then you see no Moon again.
This pattern keeps repeating.

Full Moon

Last Quarter Moon

How is this pattern made?

The Moon does not make its own light.
The part of the Moon we can see
is lit by the Sun.
The dark part is not lit by the Sun.
That is why we cannot see it.

light part

dark part

The Moon is our neighbor in space.
It helps us see in the dark.
Once people used the Moon
to keep track of the days.
They saw that it took about
28 days for the Moon to
change shape.
That's how they got
the idea for months.

REVIEW

1. What is the Moon?

2. What patterns does the Moon follow?

3. Where does the Moon get its light?

4. **Observe** Look at the Moon on page 84. What shape do you see?

5. **Think and Write** Draw how the Moon changes over a month.

Why it matters

Stars help us find our way.

Science Words

stars make their own light

constellation picture in the night sky made by stars

The Stars

Have you seen the Moon in the dark night sky?
It is the largest object there.
You can see many smaller objects, too.
Do you know what they are?

EXPLORE

What can you see in the night sky?
Why can you see all these things in the dark?

What can you see in the night sky?

Is it easy to see bright objects in the dark?

What you need

- flashlight
- glowstick
- nightlight
- small objects
- *Science Journal*

What to do

1. **Predict** Guess which group each object belongs to, *Can See Easily in the Dark* or *Cannot See Easily in the Dark*.

2. Draw the objects in the *Science Journal*. Share your ideas.

3. Help the teacher sort the objects.

4. Turn out the light and test your ideas.

   SAFETY Do not shine a light at anyone's face.

What did you find out?

1. Which objects were easy to see in the dark? Why?

2. Which objects could you see just a little? Why?

87

What are stars?

Some of the objects that glow in the
night sky are stars.
Stars make their own light.
They glow because they are so hot.
We cannot feel heat from these stars.
They are far, far away.
The Explore Activity shows that some
objects make their own light.

There is one star that is closer to Earth.
We feel its heat during the day.
Do you know what it is?

That star is the Sun.

The Sun

What patterns do stars make?

Many years ago people thought the stars looked like pictures in the sky.
A picture in the night sky made by stars is called a **constellation**.
The Big Dipper is one constellation.

Brain Power

How do you think the Big Dipper got its name?

The Big Dipper

Do you know which way is north?

The Big Dipper points to the North Star.

The North Star shows you where north is.

For a long time people at sea used this star.

It helped them find their way.

REVIEW

1. What are stars?

2. Which star is closest to Earth?

3. What is a constellation?

4. **Observe** How many stars make up the Big Dipper?

5. **Think and Write** How are stars different from the Moon?

91

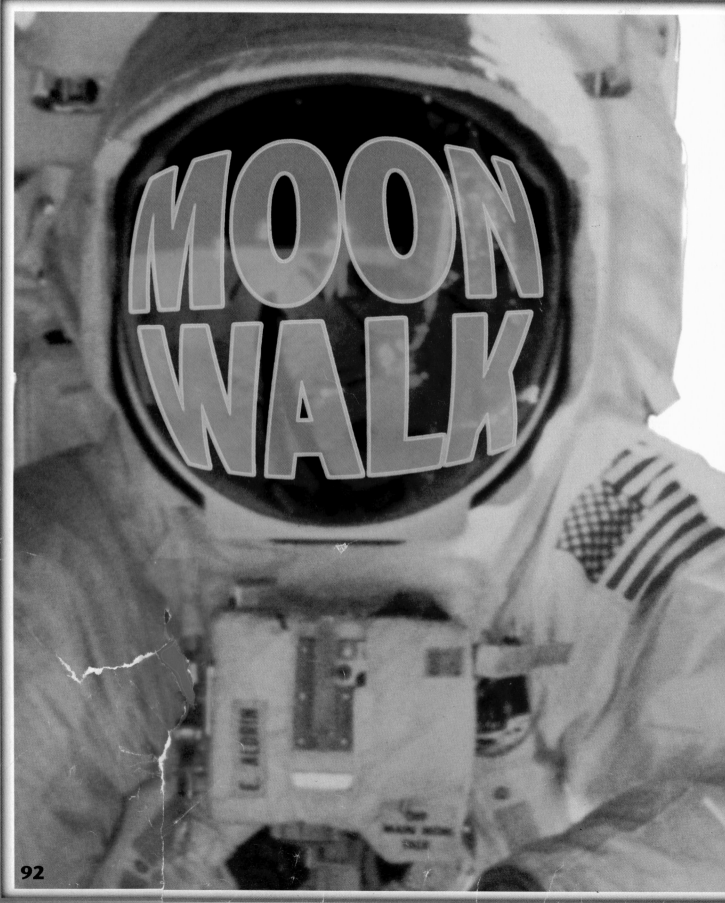

History of Science

In 1969, America sent *Apollo 11* to the Moon.

The spacecraft carried three astronauts.

Two of them walked on the Moon.

The other astronaut stayed in *Apollo 11*.

He flew around the Moon.

Then he flew everyone back to Earth!

Later, other Apollo spacecraft landed on the Moon.

Astronauts took pictures.

They brought back Moon rocks.

We learned a lot about the Moon.

DISCUSS

1. When did the first person walk on the Moon?

2. Why do you think it's hard to get to the Moon?

Use Science Words

constellation
Moon
stars

Fill in the missing science words.

1. The large ball of rock that moves around Earth is the __?__. page 82

2. Many small glowing objects in the night sky are __?__. page 88

3. A group of stars that make a picture in the night sky is a __?__. page 90

Use Science Ideas

4. Where does the Moon move? page 82

5. Where does the Moon get its light from? page 84

6. Why do the stars glow? page 88

7. Which star is closest to Earth? page 89

8. Which star heats Earth? page 89

9. Draw the Big Dipper.

10. **Observe** How does the Moon change?

PROBLEMS and PUZZLES

Big and Small Can you create a pattern using Moon shapes? Draw them on a piece of paper.

UNIT 2 REVIEW

Use Science Words

clouds shadow seasons stars temperature

1. When the day gets warmer, the ___?___ goes up.

2. It is cool in a tree's ___?___.

3. Summer and winter are both ___?___.

4. Rain falls from ___?___.

5. A constellation is a picture in the sky made up of ___?___.

Use Science Ideas

6. In which season do trees begin to lose leaves?

7. What makes the Moon shine?

8. What is the weather like today?

9. What is the Big Dipper?

10. **Infer** If the Sun is in front of you, where is your shadow?

Write in Your Journal

How does the Moon change?
Write or draw a picture.

PROBLEMS and PUZZLES

The Shadow Knows

When is the Sun's shadow longest?
Place a stick in the ground.
Trace its shadow in the morning.
Trace its shadow at noon.
Trace its shadow in the afternoon.

Make a Constellation

Make a constellation model.
Trace the pattern on a card.
Poke the holes in the card.
Darken the room.
Shine a flashlight on the pattern.

MATTER, MATTER EVERYWHERE

CHAPTER 5
LOOKING AT MATTER

Why it matters

Properties help you tell about things.

Science Words

properties how a thing looks, feels, smells, tastes or sounds

measure to find out the size or amount of something

Properties

The world is full of things to see.
Look at all these things.
How are they alike?
How are they different?

EXPLORE

How can you tell what something is?

Using your senses

How can you tell what something is by touching it? Use the objects to find out.

What you need

- **marble**
- **spoon**
- **eraser**
- **penny**
- **wooden block**
- **walnut in shell**
- **lunch bag**
- *Science Journal*

What to do

1. Put all the things in the bag. Take one out.

2. Your partner tries to find the same thing in his or her bag without looking. Your partner can only use touch.

3. **Compare** Have your partner put this object next to yours. Are they alike? Write in the *Science Journal*.

4. Now let your partner pick first.

What did you find out?

1. What helped you find the same object?

2. **Conclude** What makes some things feel different?

99

How do you use your senses?

The Explore Activity shows how to tell things apart by touch.

How an object looks, feels, smells, tastes or sounds is called its properties.

These properties can help you tell about an object.

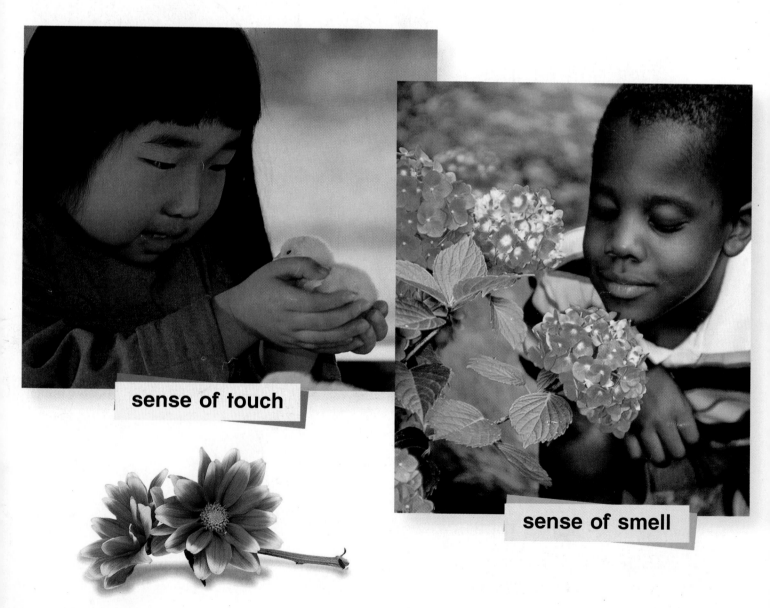

sense of touch

sense of smell

The spoon felt smooth.
The marble felt heavy.
Light, heavy, smooth, and rough
are all properties.
What other properties does the
marble have?

sense of taste

sense of hearing

How do we measure?

How much water is in the glass?
How hot is the soup?
How long is the book?
You can **measure** to find out the size or amount of something.
You use numbers when you measure something.

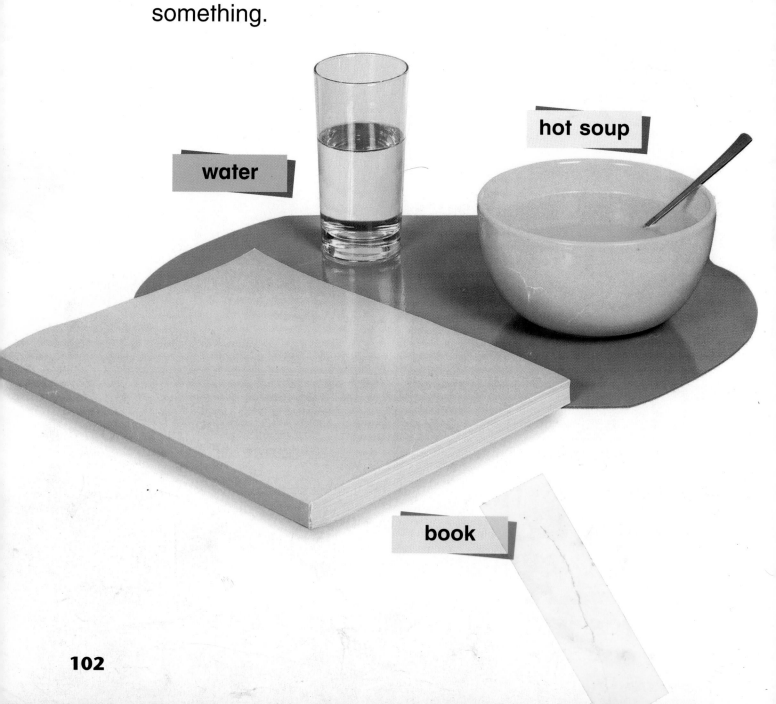

water

hot soup

book

Measure

In this activity you will measure your desk using different things.

> **What you need**
> - paper clips
> - pencils
> - *Science Journal*

What to do

1. Line the paper clips end-to-end the long way across your desk.

2 **Measure** Count how many paper clips you use. Write that number in the *Science Journal.*

3. **Predict** How many pencils will line up across your desk?

4. **Measure** Use pencils to measure your desk. Write down that number.

What did you find out?

1. **Identify** How did you measure across your desk?

2. **Explain** Are the number of paper clips and pencils the same? Why or why not?

What properties do you see?

How many things do you see?
Which of these are shiny?
Which are hard?
Which are soft?
How do you know?

Properties can help you tell
one thing from another.
You see a baby animal.
You touch its soft fur.
You hear it meow.
You know it's a kitten!

REVIEW

1. What are properties?

2. What do you use to observe the properties of an object?

3. What do you find out when you measure?

4. **Measure** How could you measure how long something is?

5. **Think and Write** What are some properties of a rock?

Topic 2

Why it matters

Our whole world is made of matter.

Science Words

matter what all things are made of

mass how much matter is in an object

Matter

How are these things alike? They are made up of a certain amount of matter. Even you are made of matter!

EXPLORE

Why do some things feel heavier than others?

How much matter?

Compare these objects to find out.

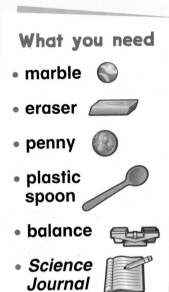

What you need

- marble
- eraser
- penny
- plastic spoon
- balance
- *Science Journal*

What to do

1. Hold each object. Which has the most matter? Which has the least?

2. **Predict** Line the objects up in order from the most to least matter. Write your prediction in the *Science Journal.*

3. **Contrast** Place the marble and spoon on the balance. Which is heavier? Write the results.

4. **Contrast** Place other pairs on the balance. Write the results.

What did you find out?

1. Did the biggest object feel the heaviest?

2. **Conclude** Which object is made up of the most matter?

What are things made of?

Matter is what all things are made of.
Bikes, balls, and boxes are made of matter.
Ants, plants, and elephants are made
of matter.
You are made of matter.

Matter can be measured.
The Explore Activity shows that the marble
is heavier than the spoon.
The marble has more **mass**.
Mass tells how much matter is in an object.
A heavier object has more mass.

NATIONAL GEOGRAPHIC

FUNtastic Facts

The blue whale is huge.
It is the biggest animal.
It has the mass of 30 elephants!
What else has that much mass?

What are properties of matter?

All matter takes up space.
A toy box takes up space.
Toys take up space.
Even you take up space.
Taking up space is a property of matter.

Matter is important.
Without it there would be no
Earth and no houses, food,
or toys.
Without it there would be
no you!

REVIEW

1. What is matter?

2. Which has more matter in it?

A B

3. What is one property of matter?

4. **Measure** How can you prove that a marble has more mass than a penny?

5. **Think and Write** Think of a small object that has more mass than a bigger object. Name them.

W rld of SCIENCE

Rocks, Rocks, Rocks

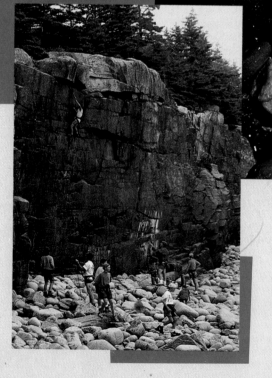

Rocks come in many sizes.
Boulders are very big.
Pebbles are very small.
They look different, but they
are all rocks.

Earth Science Link

Pumice is a rock that floats!

There are many kinds of rocks.
Some are rough, and some
are smooth.
Some rocks are colorful.
Some can be pulled by a magnet.

Many kinds of buildings
are made of rocks.
Bridges and streets can be
built with rocks, too.

Discuss

1 How are the rocks in the pictures different?

2 Name something that's made with rocks.

Use Science Words

properties
mass
matter
measure

1. You can tell how a thing looks, feels, smells, or tastes by its ___?___. page 100

2. The amount of matter in an object is its ___?___. page 109

3. You use numbers to ___?___. page 102

4. All things are made of ___?___. page 108

Use Science Ideas

5. Which has more matter, an ant or a dog? page 109

6. Name two objects with the same properties. pages 100–101

7. List 2 properties of a cat. pages 100–104

8. Why is a marble heavier than a spoon? pages 102–103

9. List 3 properties of a soccer ball. page 100

10. **Measure** What could you use to measure how long something is?

PROBLEMS and PUZZLES

Two from One Make a clay rope. Measure it. Cut it in two. Measure each piece. How did the rope change? Use a balance to compare mass.

CHAPTER 6
LET'S COMPARE
MATTER

Why it matters

You use solids every day.

Science Word

solid has a shape and a size

Solids

What is happening to the cars? How will the shape of the cars change?

EXPLORE

Could the cars change shape on their own?

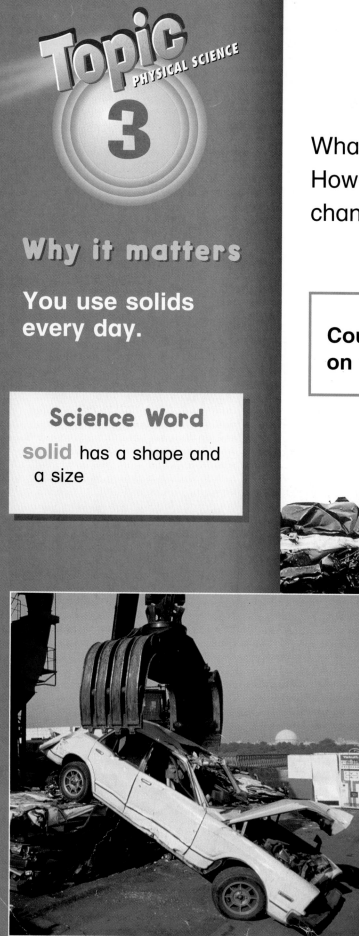

Do solid objects change shape?

Do this activity with a penny and a spoon to find out.

What you need

- penny
- spoon
- cup
- lunch bag
- *Science Journal*

What to do

1. Trace the shape of the penny and spoon in the *Science Journal.*

2. **Observe** Place the penny in the cup. Look at it. Remove it. Trace it.

3. **Observe** Place the spoon in the cup. Look at it. Remove it. Trace it.

4. **Observe** Now use the bag instead of the cup. Repeat steps 2 and 3.

What did you find out?

1. Did the penny or spoon change size or shape when you moved them?

2. **Predict** Would the penny or spoon keep its shape if you put it in a box?

117

What are solids?

The Explore Activity shows that the penny
and spoon are **solids**.
A solid has a shape and a size.
A solid keeps its shape and size.
It does not change its shape or size
on its own.

All solids are made of matter.
All solids take up space.
Blocks and cars are solids.
Can two cars park in the same space
at the same time?
No, because two solids cannot take up
the same space at the same time.

What are other properties of solids?

You can see and feel solids.

That helps you learn about them.

Some solids are soft.

Some are hard.

What other properties do these solids have?

You use solids every day.
You write with a pencil.
You drink with a cup.
You sit in a chair.
You read this book!

REVIEW

1. What is a solid?

2. What are all solids made of?

3. Can two solids take up the same space at the same time?

4. **Observe** List two properties solids can have.

5. **Think and Write** Which solids do you use every day?

Why it matters

We use liquids every day.

Science Word

liquid has no shape of its own

Liquids

Oops! The milk spilled.

The glass did not break.

The boy can pick up the glass.

What happened to the milk?

EXPLORE

Why can't the boy pick up the milk?

Does water have a shape?

MATH LINK

Find out if water keeps its shape.

What you need

- 2 different sized cups
- water
- *Science Journal*

What to do

1. Pour some water into one cup.

2. **Describe** Draw the shape of the water in the cup in the *Science Journal*.

3. Pour some water into the other cup. Draw the shape of the water.

4. **Compare** Are the shapes the same?

What did you find out?

1. **Observe** Does water keep the same shape?

2. **Infer** What shape does water take? How do you know?

What are liquids?

In the Explore Activity water did not keep its shape.

It had a different shape when it was in different cups.

Water is not a solid.

It is a liquid.

A liquid has no shape of its own.

A liquid takes the shape of the container it is in.

All liquids are made of matter.
All liquids take up space.
You can see and feel liquids.
You can pour a liquid from one
container to another.
What happens to the shape of
the liquid when you do?

What are properties of liquids?

Liquids have properties.
Some liquids are thick.
Other liquids are thin.
What other properties do these liquids have?

GEOGRAPHY LINK

Brain Power

What liquid covers most of Earth?

We use many liquids in our lives.
Everything we drink is a liquid.
We take baths in a liquid.
We swim in a liquid.
Rain is a liquid.

REVIEW

1. Does a liquid have its own shape?

2. What shape does a liquid take?

3. What are all liquids made of?

4. **Measure** How could you prove that liquids take up space like solids do?

5. **Think and Write** Which liquids do you drink? How are they alike? How are they different?

Why it matters

We breathe gases.

Science Word

gases have no size or shape of their own

Gases

Did you ever see such a big balloon?
It carries people up and away.
What a fun ride!

What do you think is inside the balloon?

EXPLORE ACTIVITY

Is air real?

Can you catch what you cannot see? Let's find out.

What you need

- plastic bag
- bag tie
- balloon
- *Science Journal*

What to do

1. Open the bag and wave it around.

2. Grab the open end and tie it.

3. Press on the bag.

4. **Observe** Draw the bag and write what it feels like to press on it in the *Science Journal.*

5. Blow up a balloon. Hold it shut with one hand. Repeat steps 3 and 4 for the balloon.

What did you find out?

1. **Compare** Did the bag feel the same as the balloon? Why or why not?

2. What did you trap in the bag and balloon?

What are gases?

The Explore Activity shows that air is real.
You can trap air in a balloon.
You can trap air in a bag.
You can feel the air.
You can tell that it takes
up space.

Air is made of different **gases.**
Gases have no size or shape of their own.
Gases spread out to fill all the space
they can.
All gases are made of matter.
All gases take up space.

What are properties of gases?

You cannot see most gases.
That is one of their properties.
You can see what air does when
the wind blows.
You can feel air in your hair!

There are gases all
around you.
They make up air.
You breathe air.
You need air to live.

REVIEW

1. What is air made of?

2. What do gases take up?

3. How do you know gases are around you?

4. **Infer** How could you use a kite to prove air is real?

5. **Think and Write** Some toys are filled with air. Make a list of toys that need air.

133

Topic 6

PHYSICAL SCIENCE

Why it matters

Heat can change solids and liquids.

Science Word

melt change from a solid to a liquid

Matter Can Change

Look at the snowman.
What is it made of?
Is it a solid?
How can you tell?

EXPLORE

What will happen to the snowman?

Can a solid change to a liquid?

Ice is a solid. What happens to ice in a warm place?

What you need

- ice cube
- cup
- *Science Journal*

What to do

1. Write your name on the cup.

2. Place the ice cube in the cup.

3. Place the cup in a sunny or a warm place.

4. **Observe** Wait 15 minutes. See what happens to the ice cube.

5. **Record** Write what happens in the *Science Journal.*

What did you find out?

1. What happened to the ice cube?

2. **Infer** What made it happen?

What is melting?

The Explore Activity shows that ice can change to liquid water.
To do this the ice must melt.
To melt means to change from a solid into a liquid.
What is melting here?

What made the ice melt?

Heat did.

Heat can make things get warmer.

Heat can make things change.

Heat can change a solid into a liquid.

What makes the ice cream melt?

What else can heat do?

Heat can also make liquids change.
Heat from the Sun warms the
water in puddles.
The water changes into a gas.
You can't see this gas.
It spreads up to the clouds.
The gas changes back to water.
The water in clouds may fall as rain.

If solids could not change,
snow and ice would never melt.
If liquids could not change,
puddles would never dry.
What else would never dry?

REVIEW

1. What happens when a solid melts?

2. What causes ice to melt?

3. What can heat do?

4. **Infer** What causes a snowman to melt?

5. **Think and Write** Where does the water from puddles go?

139

Making Colorful CRAYONS

What shape is a crayon?

Is it long and thin?

Not always!

2 Colored powder is mixed in. Each tub of wax gets one color.

1 Crayons start as solid wax. The heated wax becomes a liquid. Then it can be poured.

140

3 The hot wax is poured into a mold. The mold has little tubes.

4 The wax in each tube cools. It turns back into a solid. Now it's a crayon!

5 A label is glued around each crayon. A crayon of each color goes into a box. It's time to color!

DISCUSS

1. Is very hot wax a solid? Why or why not?

2. How could crayons be made into balls or other shapes?

141

Use Science Words

| gas |
| liquid |
| melt |
| solid |

1. Matter that has no size or shape of its own is a ___?___. page 131

2. Matter that has a shape and size is a ___?___. page 118

3. To change a solid into a liquid you can ___?___ it. page 136

4. Matter that has no shape of its own is a ___?___. page 124

Use Science Ideas

5. Is a computer a solid? pages 118–120

6. List two properties of a rock. pages 118–120

7. Can two children stand in the same spot at the same time? page 119

8. Does juice have its own shape? page 124

9. How do you know air is real? pages 129-132

10. **Infer** When a puddle dries, what happens to the water? page 138

PROBLEMS and PUZZLES

Easy, But Hard Choose five rocks. How can you test which one is the hardest? Line the rocks up from the hardest to the least hard.

Use Science Words

> gases matter measure melt properties

1. You find out how big a thing is when you ___?___.

2. Fuzzy, small, and black are some ___?___.

3. Everything is made of ___?___.

4. Balloons are filled with ___?___.

5. Heat can make ice ___?___.

Use Science Ideas

6. Is a penny a solid, a liquid, or a gas?

7. A flag waves. What moves it?

8. Which has more matter, a bike or a bus?

9. What are some different liquids?

10. **Measure** How wide is this page? Use paper clips.

Write in Your Journal

What do you see?
Write about it.

PROBLEMS and PUZZLES

Hands, Pencils, and Clips

Dan used different objects to measure his book.
The chart shows the objects Dan used.
How many hands long was the book?
Which object did Dan need the fewest of to measure?
How many paper clips long was the book?

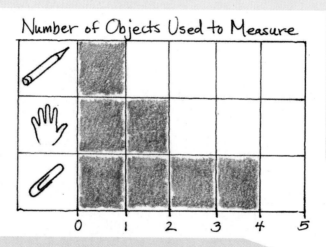

Number of Objects Used to Measure

Finger Paints

Take two colors of paint.
Mix them together.
What property changed?

144

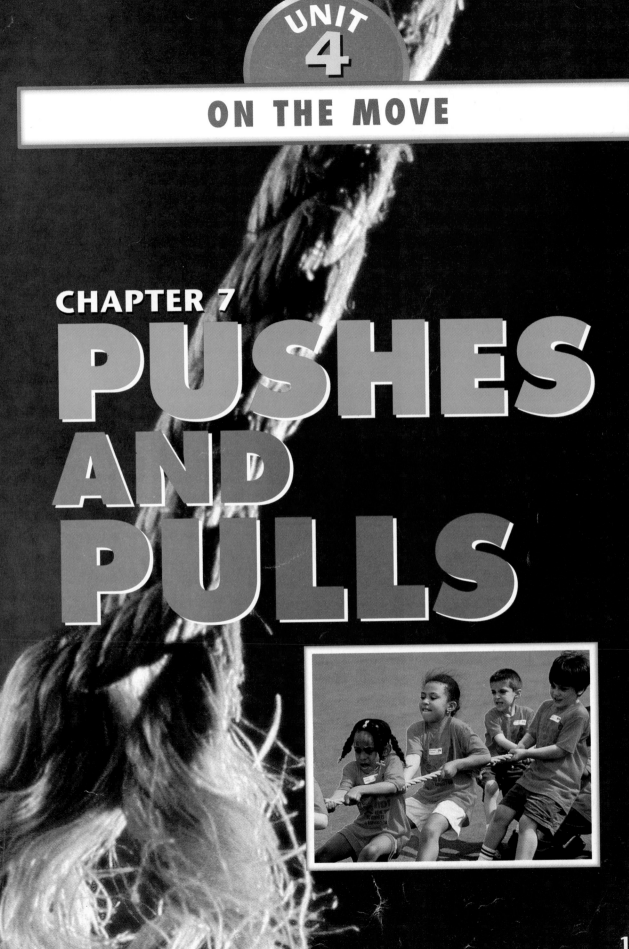

CHAPTER 7
PUSHES
AND
PULLS

Why it matters

Position words can help you.

Science Words

move to go from one place to another

position where an object is

communicate to talk, write, or draw

Position

What do you think happened here? Is the cat in trouble again? Did something move?

EXPLORE

How can you tell when something has moved? What is different?

EXPLORE ACTIVITY

What moved?

Find out if something has moved.

What to do

1. Have your partner put some objects on your desk.

2. **Observe** Look at the objects. Remember where they are.

3. Now close your eyes. Your partner will move one object.

4. Open your eyes. Tell which object you think was moved. Record in the *Science Journal*.

5. Take turns. Play this game 3 more times.

What you need

- small objects

- *Science Journal*

What did you find out?

How could you tell which object was moved?

What Happened?

The Explore Activity shows that you can
move objects.
Move means to go from one place
to another.

The objects moved from one **position**
to another.
Position is the place where an object is.

One child is inside the circle.
One child is outside the circle.

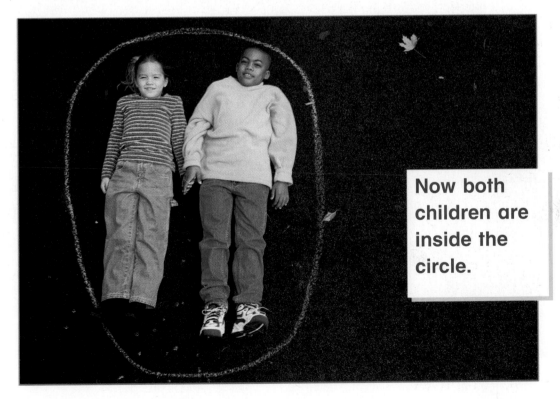

Now both children are inside the circle.

Did one child change position?
How can you tell?

Where are the animals?

Which animal is inside its mother's pouch?
Which animal is next to its mother?
The words inside and next to are
position words.
They help you tell where something is.
They help you to **communicate**.
You can communicate by talking, writing
or drawing.

Polar bear and cub

Kangaroo and its joey

Communicate

How can position words help you?

What you need
- pencil
- ball of clay
- *Science Journal*

What to do

1. Place the pencil and the clay in front of you.

2. Your teacher will tell you how to move them.

3. Which position words helped you know where to move them? Write the words in the *Science Journal.*

What did you find out?

1. How did the position words help you?

2. **Communicate** What are some other position words?

How does she move?

What happened here?
How do you know?

Position words help you every day.
They help you find things.
They help you tell others where things are.
They help you know where to go.

REVIEW

1. What is position?

2. What does move mean?

3. How can an object change its position?

4. **Communicate** Draw a picture of a cat under a table.

5. **Think and Write** Draw an object in one place. Show how it changes position.

Why it matters

Forces make things move in different ways.

Science Words

push move an object away

pull move an object closer

force what makes an object move

Objects Move

Have you ever played this game?

It is called soccer.

It is a lot of fun!

The ball moves very fast.

What makes the ball move so fast?

EXPLORE

What can make an object move? How many ways can you think of?

How can you move an object?

Let's find some ways to move objects.

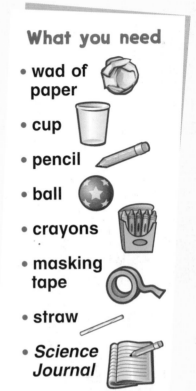

What you need

- wad of paper
- cup
- pencil
- ball
- crayons
- masking tape
- straw
- *Science Journal*

What to do

1. **Observe** Push an object with your hand. Does it move? Write in the *Science Journal*.
   SAFETY: Push gently.

2. Put tape where it stops.

3. **Observe** Use the straw. Blow gently on the same object. Does it move?

4. Put tape where it stops.

5. Try it with different objects.

What did you find out?

1. How did you move the objects?

2. **Compare** Which objects moved farther with your hand? Which objects moved farther with the straw?

How do objects move?

To move the cart, you could **push** it.
To push means to move an object
away from you.
The boy is pushing the cart.

The Explore Activity shows you can
move objects with a push.

push - - - - →

To move the cart, you could pull it.
To pull means to move an object closer to you.
The mother is pulling the cart.

You can move an object with a push or a pull.
A push or pull is called a force.
A force can make an object move.

pull

Why doesn't the box move?

Sometimes it takes a strong force
to make an object move.

NATIONAL GEOGRAPHIC

FUNtastic Facts

Magnets can pull some things.
They can pull paper clips.
Try it. Use different magnets.
Which magnet pulls farthest?

The ride goes round and round.
You push the bars.
You pull yourself up.
Then you can move round and round!

REVIEW

1. What can make an object move?

2. What does push mean?

3. What does pull mean?

4. **Communicate** Tell what is happening here.

5. **Think and Write** What did you move with a push today? Make a list.

Why it matters

Parts help objects move.

Science Words

part piece of an object

whole all the parts together

What Parts Are

Have you gone on a trip?
What did you take with you?

Jamie is going on a trip.
She has to carry her own bag.

EXPLORE

**Which bag is easier to carry?
How do you know?**

How do parts help things move?

You can add parts to a toy to change how it moves.

What you need
- toy car
- tape
- *Science Journal*

What did you find out?

1. Push the car.

2. Put tape where it stops.

3. Push it 3 more times. Start each time in the same place.
   Tape where it stops each time.

4. Now add wheels to the car.

5. Push it again. Tape where it stops.

What did you find out?

1. How did you change the car?

2. **Compare** Which moved farther? How do you know?

How do parts help things move?

The Explore Activity shows that wheels can change the way a toy moves.
The wheels are parts.
A part is a piece of an object.

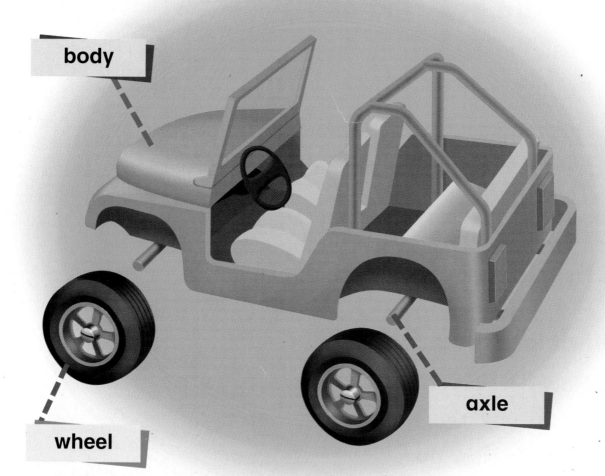

body

wheel

axle

The body of the car is one part.
The wheels are its other parts.
All the parts together make a whole.

How do the parts help the car move?

What parts do you see here?
How do all the parts help the boat to move?

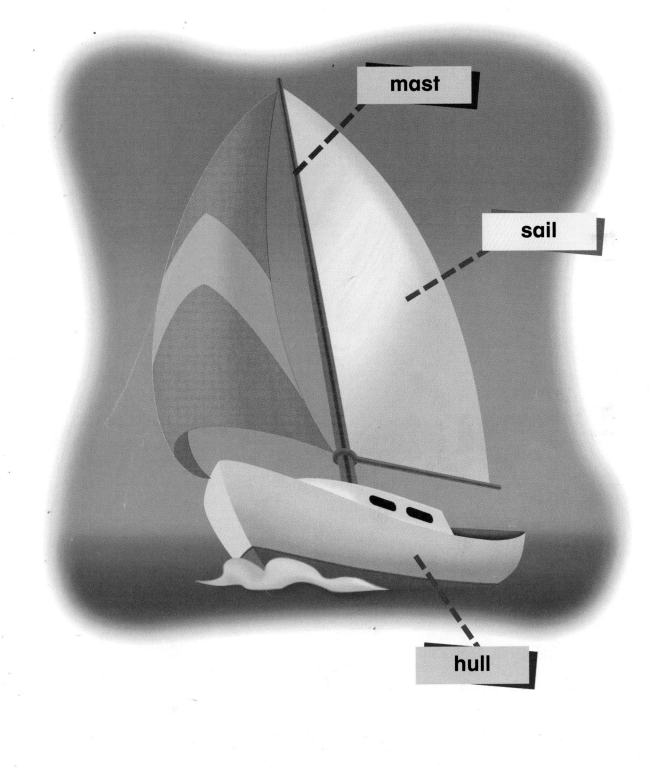

mast

sail

hull

What made it move?

The wheels are parts of these things.
The wheels help these things move.
What else do you need to make
these things move?

You can add parts to change
the way things move.
How do the training wheels help
the child ride the bike?

REVIEW

1. What is a part?

2. What is a whole?

3. What makes objects move?

4. **Communicate** Draw a sailboat. Label the parts. How do the parts help it move?

5. **Think and Write** What do you wish had wheels on it? Why?

Why it matters

Parts work together to help things move.

Parts Work Together

Do you want to fly a kite?
Here we go!

Watch the kite sail through the air.
See the tail as it waves goodbye.
Hold on tight to the string!

EXPLORE

**What are the parts of a kite?
How does a kite move?**

Can a kite fly without a tail? ART LINK

A kite flies in the air. Does it need a tail to fly?

What to do

1. Trace the kite pattern onto 2 pieces of paper. Tape the pieces together.

2. Cut out the kite and color it in.

3. Use a pencil tip to make 2 holes at the corners. Thread the string through the holes and knot it.

4. Fold the sides of the kite up.

5. Fly the kite.

6. Now add a tail and fly it.

What you need

- kite pattern
- scissors
- crayons
- string
- crepe paper
- pencil
- *Science Journal*

What did you find out?

1. Did the kite fly better with or without the tail?

2. **Infer** What makes a kite fly?

How do parts work together?

In the Explore Activity, the kite flew.
All the parts worked together.

Look at these parts.
What can each part do?
What could you make if you put all the parts together?

frame

running board

handle bars

wheel

All the parts together make a scooter.
Which parts roll?
Which part could you stand on?
Only a force will make the scooter move.

What kind of force does the girl use?

Why Doesn't It Work?

Would the scooter work with one wheel?
Would it work with no frame?
A scooter needs all of its parts to work the way it should.
Which objects here are missing a part?

Most objects are made
of many parts.
Each part does a job.
All the parts work together.
They make a whole.
Even your body is
made of many parts.

REVIEW

1. How does a scooter move?

2. What might happen if a toy is missing a part?

3. Would a scooter work without a wheel?

4. **Observe** Will the bicycle work? Why or why not?

5. **Think and Write** Name a body part.

Up with the Wind

What makes a kite fly?
The wind!
It pushes and lifts a kite.
Let out some string to send
a kite up higher.
Wooden sticks shape a kite.
Some kites have tails.

Look at these
different kinds of kites.
Find the parts that are the same.

A sailboat uses the wind, too.
The large sails catch the wind.
The wind moves the boat forward.
What happens if you turn a sail?
You change the direction the
sailboat is going.

Discuss

1 What might happen to a kite that has no tail?

2 What other things can the wind move?

CHAPTER 7 REVIEW

Use Science Words

communicate
force
move
part
position
pull
push
whole

1. The place where an object is at is called its ___?___. page 148

2. A piece of an object is a ___?___. page 162

3. To move an object away, you could ___?___ it. page 156

4. A push or a pull is called a ___?___. page 157

5. All parts make a ___?___. page 162

6. To bring an object closer, you could ___?___ it. page 157

7. To go from one place to another is to ___?___. page 148

8. Talking is one way to ___?___. page 150

Use Science Ideas

9. What kind of force do you use to move a scooter? pages 156-157

10. **Communicate** Draw a cat on top of a box.

PROBLEMS and PUZZLES

Smart Move Use pencils to move a book. Put one end of a pencil under a book. Put another pencil under the first. Push down on the first pencil. What happens?

CHAPTER 8
WHAT MOVES?

Why it matters

Parts help living things move.

How Living Things Move

What if nothing moved?
Everywhere you look, you see things move.
People move.
Animals move.

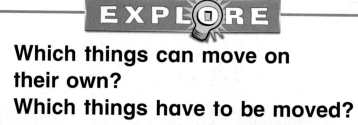

EXPLORE

Which things can move on their own?
Which things have to be moved?

My puppet and me

How are you and a puppet alike?
How are you different from the puppet?

What you need
- puppet parts
- fasteners
- string
- straw
- *Science Journal*

What to do

1. Decorate the puppet parts to look like you.

2. Fasten the puppet together.

3. Pull the string. What happens? Record in the *Science Journal*.

4. Move in different ways. Jump. Hop.

5. Make the puppet move in the same way.

What did you find out?

1. Which puppet parts can move?

2. **Compare** How are you and the puppet alike? How are you different?

177

How do living things move?

You move your own body when you jump, run, or hop around.
The Explore Activity shows that a puppet cannot move by itself.
It has to be moved.

Many things are moving in this park.
Count how many move by themselves.
Count how many have to be moved.

How do animals move?

Living things move in many ways.
The lion runs and jumps.
The snake zigzags.
The dolphin swims.
The butterfly flies.
How do you move?

butterfly

lion

snake

dolphin

Animals use many body parts to move.
The parts work together.
They may push and they may pull.
Without a force, animals cannot move.
Which parts do you use to move?

REVIEW

1. How does a puppet move?

2. How does a butterfly move?

3. How do you move?

4. **Observe** What can move on its own? What has to be moved?

5. **Think and Write** How many different ways did you move today?

Why it matters

Living things need to move to stay alive.

Why Living Things Move

How is the bird helping its babies?

The baby birds are hungry.

They do not know how to fly yet.

They cannot find their own food.

EXPLORE

Why do living things move?

How do birds get food?

What to do

What you need

- rubber bands
- *Science Journal*

1. Your teacher hides rubber bands. The rubber bands are worms.

2. Let a player be the parent bird. Let 3 players be baby birds.

3. **Model** One bird finds worms and brings them back to its babies.
   SAFETY: Don't put the worms in your mouth.

4. Write the number of worms the bird found in the *Science Journal*.

5. Try it again. Now have 2 birds look for food.

6. Write the number of worms each bird found this time.

What did you find out?

1. What did the bird have to do to find food?

2. **Infer** When was it easier for the bird to find food?

Why do animals move?

In the Explore Activity, the bird moves to find food.

Animals move to meet their needs.

Needs are what living things must have to stay alive.

Food, water, and shelter are needs.

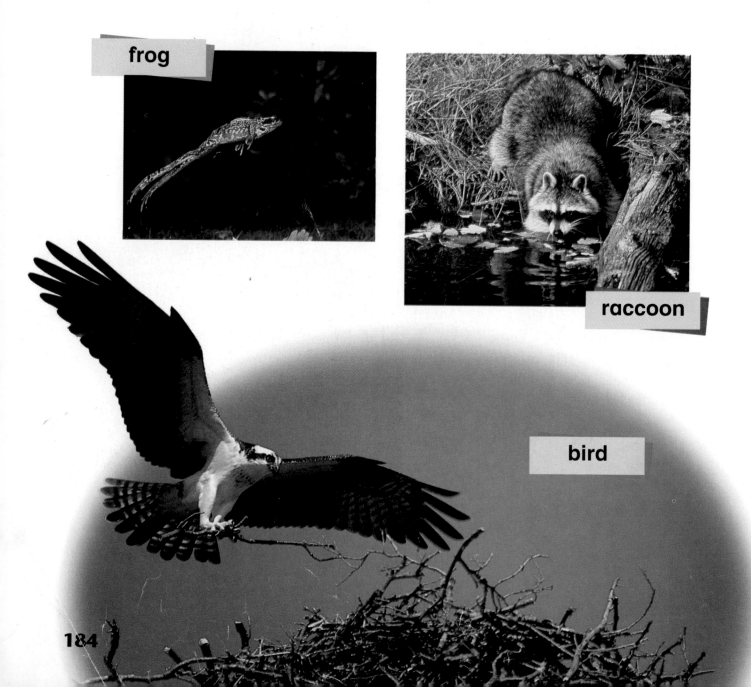

frog

raccoon

bird

Some animals move into the
sunshine to warm up.

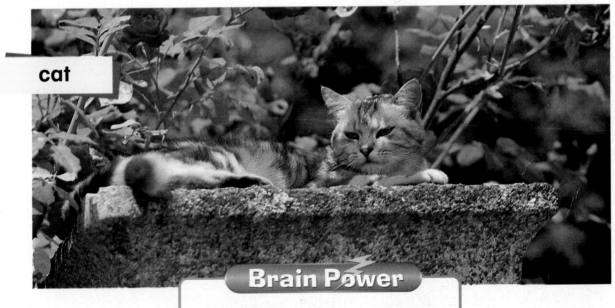

lizard

They move into the shade to cool off.

cat

Brain Power

Why else might animals
move?

Why do you move?

Do you move to find something to eat?
Do you move to find something to drink?
What other needs do you meet by moving?
Do you move when you play?

Animals move to get what they need.
Moving helps them stay alive.
Moving helps you stay alive, too.
What would the world be like
if nothing moved?

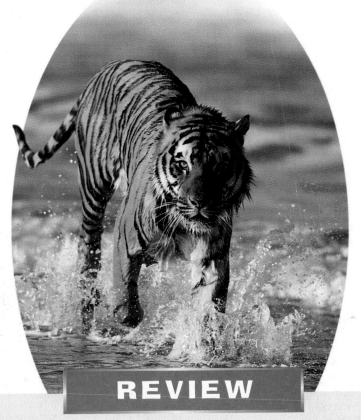

REVIEW

1. What are needs?

2. Why do animals move?

3. Why do people move?

4. **Infer** Why is the tiger at the stream?

5. **Think and Write** Did you have to move today? Why?

187

GET MOVING

Who's the fastest land animal?

The cheetah is.

Cheetahs live in Africa.

They are endangered animals.

The antelope runs fast, too.

It lives in Africa.

Antelopes can run away from

hungry mountain lions!

**Cheetah
112 km (70 mi)**

Horses live in many places.

Some run fast in races.

Some run just for fun.

The fox lives in the woods.

It runs to catch mice and rabbits to eat!

DISCUSS

1. Which is faster, the cat or the fox?

2. Why do some animals move fast?

Person
45 km (28 mi)

House cat
48 km (30 mi)

Fox
67 km (42 mi)

Antelope
98 km (61 mi)

RUNNING NUMBERS
The numbers tell how fast each animal can run in an hour.

The hummingbird flies fast. Its wings can move up to 80 times in one second!

189

Use Science Ideas

1. What are three needs of animals? page 184

2. What do you need to stay alive? pages 184–186

3. Which thing can move by itself? pages 178–179

   a)   b)

4. Name an animal that can fly. page 180

5. Name an animal that can hop. page 184

6. Name an animal that can swim. page 180

7. What are some ways you can move? page 180

8. Why do you move? page 186

9. Why do animals move? pages 184–185

10. **Communicate** Draw a picture of an animal that can fly.

PROBLEMS and PUZZLES

Push and Pull Look around the room. What can you move just by pulling? What can you move just by pushing? Make a list.

Use Science Words

move	needs	part	pull	push

1. To move an object away, you __?__ it.

2. A wheel is __?__ of a bicycle.

3. When you go to another place, you __?__.

4. To stay alive, an animal __?__ food.

5. To bring an object closer, you __?__ it.

Use Science Ideas

6. Name one way you can communicate.

7. How does a fish move?

8. What do dogs need when they are thirsty?

9. What part of your body helps you to walk?

10. **Communicate** Draw a picture of a ball on top of a table.

Write in Your Journal

What do you see?
Write about it.

PROBLEMS and PUZZLES

Traffic Jam

What position does each thing have?
The yellow car is in front.
The red bird is above.
What are the positions of other things?
Can you describe each position?

Animal Race

On your mark.
Get set.
GO!
The animals are having a race.
Which animal will crawl to the finish line?
Which animal will run?
Hop? Flutter? Slither? Fly? Swim? Climb?

192

CHAPTER 9
DOWN
BY THE
POND

Why it matters

A pond is a home to many plants and animals.

Science Words

pond water with land all around

habitat where animals and plants live and grow

classify put things into groups

The Pond

Have you ever seen a pond? Look at this picture. Where do you see plants growing? How many animals can you find? What part of the pond are the animals in?

Do you think a pond could make a good home?

Why is a pond a good home?

In this activity you will find out why some plants and animals live in ponds.

What you need

- Picture cards
- *Science Journal*

What to do

1. **Observe** Look at the cards.

2. Where do you see each animal?

3. What is each animal doing? Write your answer in the *Science Journal*.

What did you find out?

1. **Infer** What does each animal find at the pond?

2. **Infer** Why is a pond a good home for pond animals?

What is a pond?

A pond is water with land all around it.
A pond is smaller than a lake. It is not as
deep as a lake.

Many plants and animals live in ponds.
The Explore Activity shows some of them.
Some plants grow in the middle of the
pond. Others grow closer to the shore.

Where are the animals living in this pond?
The place where animals and plants live
and grow is called their habitat. A habitat
gives animals and plants all they need to live.

Plants need sunlight, water, and room to
grow. Animals need food, water, and
shelter.

How are pond animals alike?

You can **classify** animals by the number of legs they have. To classify means to put things into groups.

Which animals have four legs? Which animals have six legs? Can you classify these animals another way?

Water Strider

Raccoon

Turtle

Dragonfly

SKILL BUILDER

Classify

In this activity you will find different ways to classify pond animals.

What to do

1. **Classify** Put the cards into two groups: animals that only live in water and animals that only live on land. Write the groups in the *Science Journal*.

2. **Classify** Make a group of new animals that live in both places.

3. **Classify** Group the animals by the way they move.

4. Find a new way to group the animals.

What did you find out?

1. **Compare and Contrast** How are the animals alike? How are they different?

2. How did you classify the animals?

Who lives at a pond?

Animals live in every part of a pond. Clams live in the mud. Fish swim in the water. Insects walk on top of the water. Birds build nests in the plants. Turtles crawl on shore. Frogs hop on lily pads.

Water Strider

NATIONAL GEOGRAPHIC

FUNtastic Facts

Some beetles can dive.
They eat insects and fish.
They won't bite you!
What eats beetles?

A pond is home to many plants. A pond is home to many animals. It is a place for them to grow, get food, and live.

You have a home. Why is your home important to you?

REVIEW

1. What is a pond?

2. What is a habitat?

3. Why is a pond a good habitat for an animal?

4. **Classify** Sort pond animals into 2 groups: animals that have wings and animals that do not have wings. Make a list.

5. **Think and Write** Draw a pond. Show animals that live in different parts of the pond.

Why it matters

Nonliving things help make up a pond.

Science Word

nonliving things
things that do not grow, breathe, or need food

Nonliving Parts of the Pond

Did you ever look closely at a pond? Now is your chance!

Look at the water. What do you see there? What else do you see in this picture? Can you tell the parts of a pond?

EXPLORE

What would you need to make a pond?

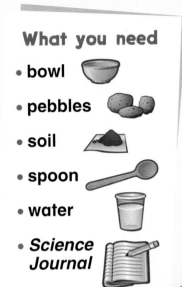
How can you make a pond?

In this activity you will make a model of a pond.

What you need

- bowl
- pebbles
- soil
- spoon
- water
- *Science Journal*

What to do

1. Put some rocks in the bottom of the bowl.

2. Add soil. Push the soil down.

3. Pat down the soil with a little water.

4. Dig out a small hole in the soil.

5. Add water to the hole.
   SAFETY Wash your hands.

What did you find out?

1. What makes up your pond?

2. What is the shape of your pond?

What is not alive at a pond?

The Explore Activity shows what makes up a pond. A pond is made of more than water. At the bottom there are mud, soil, sand, and rocks of many sizes.

Rocks, soil, water, and sunlight are **nonliving things**. Nonliving things do not grow, breathe, or need food.

Plants need nonliving things to grow. They need water and sunlight. Most plants also need soil. A pond has all these things.

Pond plants grow in the soil on the bottom of a pond. A pond is not deep. Sunlight can reach leaves that grow under the water.

Who makes ponds?

People dig ponds on farms and in yards. Beavers also make ponds. They build a dam across a stream. The dam traps water for the pond. Then the beavers build a home in their pond.

Beaver

Ponds come in all sizes and shapes. Some have sandy soil. Some have muddy soil. Without nonliving things, pond plants could not grow. Pond animals would have no place to live. Which nonliving things do you need to live?

REVIEW

1. What are the nonliving parts of a pond?

2. Where do plants grow in a pond?

3. How do beavers make a pond?

4. **Classify** Sort the parts of a pond into living and nonliving things.

5. **Think and Write** Why is a pond a good habitat for plants?

Why it matters

Pond animals stay alive, even in winter.

Science Word

freeze to change from a liquid to a solid

Ponds Change

Which season do you think it is here? When the seasons change, the pond changes, too. What has happened to this pond? How has it changed?

Where are all the animals now? Can some animals still live in the pond?

Where do pond animals live in winter?

Let's make a pond and find out!

What you need
- small bowl
- water
- pencil
- *Science Journal*

What to do

1. Fill your bowl with water.

2. Put the bowl in the freezer for a little while.

3. **Predict** Write what you think will happen in the *Science Journal.*

4. **Observe** Take the bowl out of the freezer. What happened?

5. Make a hole in the ice with a pencil.
   ▨ SAFETY Be careful with the pencil.

What did you find out?

1. What part of the water turned to ice?

2. What is under the ice?

3. **Infer** How can pond animals stay alive in a pond in winter?

How does a pond change in winter?

A pond changes from season to season. In winter the top part of the pond may **freeze**. To freeze means to change from a liquid to a solid. The Explore Activity shows how water changes to ice.

Fish can still live in the water below. Some insects can, too. The ice keeps them safe from the cold weather. Frogs and turtles bury themselves in the mud. They sleep there all winter.

Some animals leave the pond for the winter. Ducks and other birds fly south to warmer places. Some plants die and others lose their leaves. Animals that stay must work hard to find food during the winter months.

How does a pond change in spring?

When spring returns the pond comes alive again. The days get longer and warmer. Buds open and leaves grow. Frogs and turtles wake up and dig out of the mud. Birds fly in to make nests and lay eggs. There is plenty of food for pond animals now.

In cold places, water saves pond animals. Only the top part of the water freezes in winter. The animals can stay alive under the ice until spring. Never walk or skate on a pond. The ice is thin!

REVIEW

1. How does a pond change in winter?

2. What happens to pond frogs in winter?

3. What happens to pond fish in winter?

4. **Classify** Group pond animals in winter by where they live.

5. **Think and Write** Tell how a pond changes in spring.

213

Water, Water Everywhere

All living things need water.
Where do we get our water?
It starts as rain or snow.
Rain flows downhill into streams.
Streams flow into rivers.
Rivers flow into oceans.

Geography Link

Some rain sinks
into the ground.
Sometimes people dig
wells to get water.

We use a lot of water.
Will lakes and rivers stay full?
Yes, rain and melting snow
fill them with water!

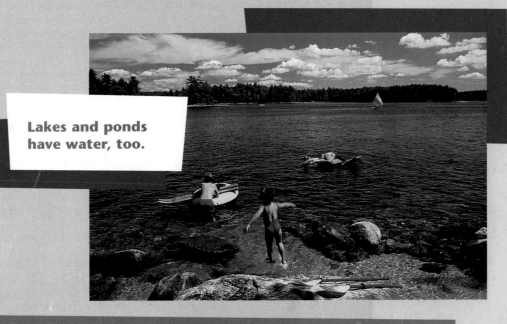

**Lakes and ponds
have water, too.**

Discuss

How do you use water?

Use Science Words

classify
freezes
habitat
nonliving thing
pond

1. Something that does not grow, breathe, or need food is a ___?___. page 204

2. Water turns to ice when it ___?___. page 210

3. Water with land all around it is a ___?___. page 196

4. Where an animal lives is its ___?___. page 197

5. To put things into groups is to ___?___. page 198

Use Science Ideas

6. Which is nonliving? page 204

   a)   b)

7. Where do plants grow at a pond? page 196

8. Why can plants grow at a pond? page 205

9. How do pond animals stay alive in winter? pages 210–211

10. **Classify** Group the nonliving and living parts of a pond. pages 204–205

PROBLEMS and PUZZLES

Fresh Catch The water in ponds is fresh water. It is not salty like sea water. Do you think the same animals and plants live in ponds as in the sea? Explain.

CHAPTER 10
THE LIVING PARTS OF A POND

Why it matters

Pond animals grow and change.

Science Word

tadpole a young frog

Animals in a Pond

What did you look like when you were a baby? Do you look the same now?

All animals grow and change. Pond animals grow and change, too.

How did this animal change?

218

How do pond animals change?

Do this activity to see how some animals change as they grow.

What you need

- Picture cards
- animal name cards
- lunch bag
- *Science Journal*

What to do

1. Pick an animal name card.

2. Put all the Picture cards in the bag.

3. Pick a card from the bag. Keep the card if it matches your animal. Put it back in the bag if it does not.

4. Play until all the cards are picked.

5. Put your cards in order to show how the animal changes as it grows. Write the order in the *Science Journal.*

What did you find out?

1. **Conclude** Do all animals look like their parents?

2. How did your animal change as it grew?

219

How does a frog change as it grows?

Frogs change as they grow.
The Explore Activity shows how they change.

1 **Frogs lay their eggs in a pond.**

2 Tadpoles **hatch from the eggs. A tadpole is a young frog. Tadpoles live in water. They swim like a fish. They breathe with gills.**

3 As a tadpole grows, it starts to change. It grows legs. It loses its tail.

4 Soon the tadpole grows into an adult frog. It can leap onto land or swim in the water. Only adult frogs can lay eggs. Now they breathe with lungs.

Why is a pond a good habitat for a frog?

How do ducks live in the pond?

The pond is a good habitat for ducks, too. Ducks use their webbed feet to swim. They feed on pond plants. They also dive into the water to eat fish and tadpoles.

The tall grasses make a safe place to build a nest. Ducklings hatch from the eggs. They swim in the pond. Their mother watches over them.

Brain Power

Why would the tall grasses be a safe place to make a nest?

As you grow up, you will change. Pond animals also change as they grow. Each animal needs food to grow. They find it in the pond. Each animal needs room to move. They find that in the pond, too.

REVIEW

1. What is a young frog?

2. What do tadpoles hatch from?

3. Where do tadpoles live?

4. **Infer** Where would an animal with webbed feet live? Why?

5. **Think and Write** Draw what frogs could find to eat at a pond.

Topic 5
LIFE SCIENCE

Why it matters

Each link in a food chain is important.

Science Word
food chain shows you what animals eat

Food at a Pond

Do you know what time it is here at the pond? It is supper time!

Can you see what the frog is eating? How do you think the frog caught its food?

EXPLORE

How do the animals of the pond catch their food? What parts of their bodies do they use?

Who catches what?

Do all pond animals get their food in the same way? Use models to help you find out.

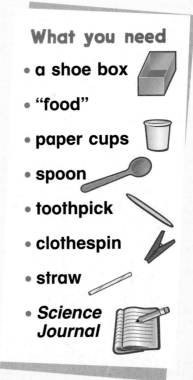

What you need

- a shoe box
- "food"
- paper cups
- spoon
- toothpick
- clothespin
- straw
- *Science Journal*

What to do

1. Mix all of the food in the shoe box.

2. Use your tool to catch the food. Put the food in the cup. Do this until you can't catch anymore.

3. Count what you caught. Write the number in the *Science Journal*.

What did you find out?

1. **Compare** Which food was easiest for you to catch?

2. Did everyone catch the same kind of food? Why or why not?

3. **Infer** Do all the animals at the pond eat the same kind of food?

225

What do pond animals eat?

The Explore Activity shows that different animals eat different foods. Ducks, tadpoles, and other pond animals eat pond plants. This food helps these animals live and grow.

READING LINK

Some pond animals are hunters. They eat other animals for food. Fishes, turtles, frogs, and birds all eat insects. Some birds eat fishes. Some insects do, too.

How does each animal catch its food?

What is a food chain?

Plants make food using sunlight. The food helps the plants grow. A tadpole eats a plant. A diving beetle eats a tadpole. The plant, tadpole, and diving beetle are links in a **food chain**. A food chain shows you what animals eat.

You can buy food in stores. Pond animals can only eat pond plants or other pond animals. That is why every link in a food chain is important. Without plants there would be no food. Without plant-eaters there would be no food for hunters.

REVIEW

1. What is a food chain?

2. Why is the Sun important in a food chain?

3. What does a tadpole eat?

4. **Classify** Pick 4 animals that live in a pond. Group those animals into hunters and plant-eaters.

5. **Think and Write** Draw a food chain for animals at a pond.

Why it matters

Animals use different ways to stay alive.

Science Word

survive to stay alive

Staying Alive

Can you spot the walking stick in this picture? Is it easy to see? A walking stick is an animal that likes to sit on leaves. How do you think it got its name?

EXPLORE

Would the walking stick be as easy to see if it were sitting on a red leaf? Why or why not?

How can color and shape keep an animal safe?

We can use model fish to find out.

What to do

1. **Observe** Look at the paper. What color fish do you see?

2. **Predict** How many fish do you think there are? Write your guess in the *Science Journal*.

3. **Observe** Look at the paper again. Tally the fish you see. Count your tally marks. Write the number.

What did you find out?

1 Which fish were easy to see? Why?

2. Which fish were hard to see? Why?

3. **Infer** Which fish might be easy for a heron to catch? Why?

How do some animals stay safe?

The color of some pond animals helps them to stay safe. The Explore Activity shows this.

The bird in the picture above is the same color as the grass.
Is the bird hard to find?
If the bird were red, would you be able to see it better?

The color of some animals helps them to survive. Survive means to stay alive.

Animals can also hide to survive. A turtle is hungry. It sees a young fish to eat. The young fish senses danger. It hides under a lily pad and does not move.

How do other animals survive?

Hiding is not the only way to survive.
Turtles and clams can pull into their
hard shells.

Other animals can move
quickly to get away.
Frogs can leap.
Birds can fly.

It's not easy for animals to stay alive. They must find food. They must find ways to keep safe. Never harm a pond animal. It might not be able to survive.

REVIEW

1. How can color help an animal survive?

2. How can not moving help an animal survive?

3. What are 2 ways animals can survive at a pond?

4. **Observe** Which animal is harder to find? Why?

Ⓐ   Ⓑ

5. **Think and Write** Pick an animal and tell how it survives in a pond.

235

The Perfect HOME

Plants and animals live all over the world.

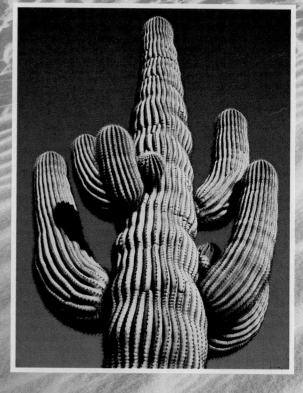

Many deserts are very hot and dry.

It almost never rains in the desert.

How do plants and animals get the water they need?

Cactus plants store it in their stems.

Geography Link

It rains almost every day in the rain forest.

Many trees and plants grow there.

Lots of different animals live there. It's the perfect place for birds, insects, and monkeys.

More plants and animals live in rain forests than in the desert. Why do you think this is?

Use Science Words

food chain
survive
tadpole

1. To stay alive means to __?__. page 233

2. A young frog is a __?__. page 220

3. Something that shows what animals eat is called a __?__. page 228

Use Science Ideas

How does each animal survive? pages 232-234

4.

5.

6.

7.

8. Draw 3 animals that could live at a pond. pages 226-227

9. Why is a pond a good habitat for a duck? page 222

10. **Classify** List 7 animals that live in a pond. Sort them into 3 groups: animals that live on land, animals that live in water, animals that live in both places. page 199

PROBLEMS and PUZZLES

Pond Club List living things and nonliving things in a pond. Cross out one thing. What happens to the other living things in the pond without it?

Use Science Words

| food chain | freeze | habitat | nonliving things | tadpole |

1. The place where a plant lives is its ___?___.

2. Things like rocks that do not grow are ___?___.

3. In winter, water in a pond may ___?___.

4. A young frog that swims like a fish is a ___?___.

5. A frog eats a fly. A fish eats the frog. The fly, frog, and fish are parts of a ___?___.

Use Science Ideas

6. Why is a pond a good habitat for a frog?

7. List 2 things all plants need to grow.

8. How do ducks survive in winter?

9. Why do some animals hide?

10. **Classify** Group 4 things at a pond into living and nonliving.

Write in Your Journal

What do you see?
Write about it.

PROBLEMS and PUZZLES

What's wrong with this pond?

Can you find the animals or things that don't belong? Explain why each animal or thing does not belong.

NO SWIMMING! SHARKS

Food Chain Hanger

Make a food chain hanger.
Write a plant or animal
on each card.
Tie the cards together.
Hang your food chain hanger
from the ceiling.

CHAPTER 11
YOU GROW AND CHANGE

Why it matters

You need things to help you grow up strong and healthy.

Growing and Changing

How will these animals change? They will grow to look like their parents.

The seasons change. The weather changes. Rocks change. Plants and animals change. Just about everything changes.

EXPLORE

Once you could not sit, stand, or walk.
How have you changed?

How have you changed?

Look at yourself to find out.

What to do

1. **Observe** Look at the pictures. How did the person change? Write the changes in the *Science Journal.*

2. Now write about you. When were you born? How long were you? How much did you weigh?

3. List things you could do as a baby.

What did you find out?

1. **Conclude** How have you changed since you were born?

2. **Infer** Will you still change? How?

243

Do you grow and change?

People grow and change as they get older. The Explore Activity shows how. How do you know that you grow?

Some clues you can see. Your clothes don't fit. You need bigger shoes. Your baby teeth fall out. Your hair and nails grow back each time you cut them.

It is easy to watch you grow on the outside. The inside of you grows, too. You can't see it, so how do you know this? There are clues.

Are you getting taller? This means that your bones are growing. Are you heavier? You weigh more when any part of you grows. Over the years your body will change a lot.

How do we use numbers?

You get bigger as you grow. Animals do, too. Numbers can tell how big animals get when they are grown up. You don't even need to see the animals. Just look at the numbers!

The chart shows how long some animals grow. Which animal is longest?

Animal	How Long?
beaver	91 centimeters
skunk	38 centimeters
raccoon	61 centimeters
cat	56 centimeters

NATIONAL GEOGRAPHIC

FUNtastic Facts

Giraffes' necks can be 6 feet long!
A giraffe has 7 neck bones.
Each bone is 11 inches long.
How long is your neck?

Use Numbers

In this activity you will use numbers to show that you have grown.

What you need

- measuring tape

- *Science Journal*

What to do

1. How long were you when you were born? Write in the *Science Journal*.

2. **Measure** Have a partner measure how tall you are. Write the number.

3. **Measure** Now measure your partner. Your partner writes the number.

What did you find out?

1. **Compare** How do your birth length and your height compare?

2. **Use Numbers** What do the numbers show?

What happens when you grow older?

Your body will keep growing until you are about 18 or 20 years old. Who do you think will keep growing in these pictures?

Your body changes as you grow old. Yet your mind can keep learning new things your whole life.

What does it take to grow up strong and healthy? It takes you. You can eat healthful foods. You can stay active. You can get plenty of rest.

REVIEW

1. Which parts of you are growing?

2. How can you tell your bones are growing longer?

3. What can you do to grow strong and healthy?

4. **Use Numbers** How many baby teeth have you lost?

5. **Think and Write** How have you changed since you were a baby? Write about it.

World of SCIENCE

Growing Up

This puppy looks like its mother, only smaller. As it grows, it will still look like its mother. Other baby animals change a lot as they grow.

A Closer Look

Did you know that a caterpillar is
really a baby butterfly?
The caterpillar eats and grows.
One day it stops eating and
holds on to a branch.
The caterpillar sheds its skin.
Underneath is a shell called
a chrysalis.
Soon the chrysalis opens.
Out comes a beautiful butterfly!

Discuss

**Think of your favorite animal. How does it
change as it grows?**

Use Science Words

weight
height

1. When you want to tell how tall you are, you give your ___?___. page 247

2. When you want to tell how heavy you are, you give your ___?___. page 243

Use Science Ideas

3. What happens to your baby teeth? page 244

4. What grow back every time you cut them? page 244

5. How do you know your bones grow? page 245

6. What will happen to you after age 18 or 20? page 248

7. Do you ever stop learning? page 248

8. What helps you grow up healthy? page 249

9. Describe what you think you will be like at age 10. page 248

10. **Use Numbers** How many teeth have you lost? page 246

PROBLEMS and PUZZLES

Thought Bubbles Keep a list of your favorite things. How often do you change your mind?

CHAPTER 12
YOU, INSIDE AND OUT

Why it matters

We need bones and muscles to move.

Science Words

skeleton a body frame made up of bones

muscle moves a bone by pulling on it

joint place where bones meet

The Inside of You

Did you ever play softball? You step up to the plate. You hold the bat tight. You lift it. Here comes the ball. You swing the bat. Whack! The ball sails away.

EXPLORE

The bat moved the ball. Do you know what moved you?

EXPLORE ACTIVITY

What makes your hand so strong?

What you need

- X-ray picture
- *Science Journal*

What to do

1. Trace your hand in the *Science Journal*.

2. **Observe** Feel your hand and fingers. Draw what is inside.

3. Compare your drawing to the picture.

What did you find out?

1. What makes your hand so strong?

2. **Infer** How are your hands and feet alike?

What holds you up?

A frame holds up a house. What holds you up? The skeleton inside you! A skeleton is a body frame made up of bones. The Explore Activity shows that bones are inside your hand. Can you feel the bones in your head, arms, and chest? How do they feel?

Your bones help give your body its shape.
Some bones help keep parts inside you
safe. When your bones grow, you grow.

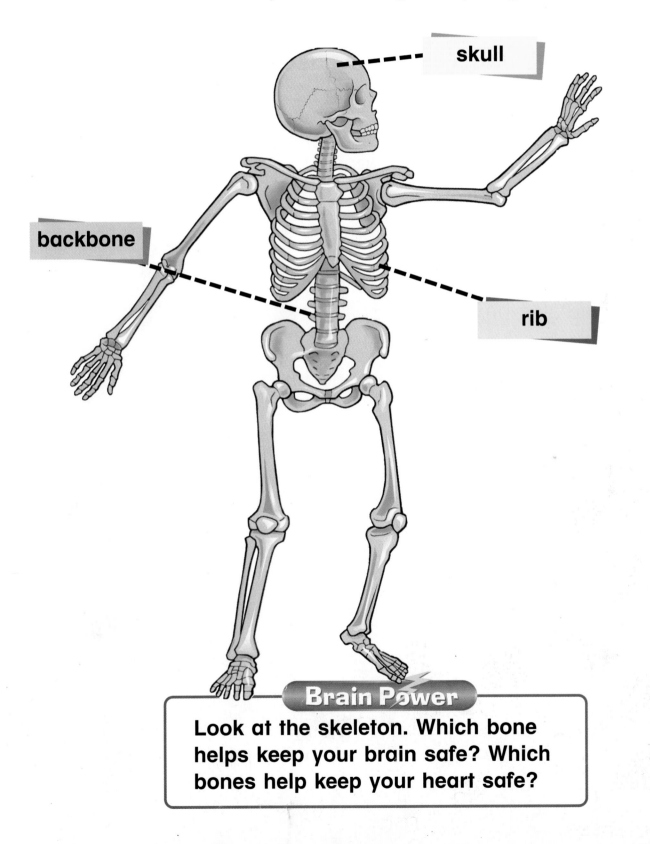

skull

backbone

rib

Brain Power

Look at the skeleton. Which bone
helps keep your brain safe? Which
bones help keep your heart safe?

What are joints and muscles?

Your bones can't move
on their own. Only your **muscles**
can move them. A muscle
moves a bone by pulling on it.
Muscles lift your leg bones
when you run.
Muscles move your hand bones
when you wave.

Muscles have other jobs, too.
They help give you shape.
They keep your bones and insides safe.

bone

Your bones are hard. They cannot bend. If they did, they would break. The places where bones meet are called joints. Joints move when muscles move bones. Bend your arm. Turn your head. Make a fist. You just used some of your many joints.

This muscle pulls on the bone. The bone moves up and the joint moves.

muscle

joint

How do you move?

When you run, what moves your legs? Your muscles do. They pull on bones in your legs. Your legs bend and unbend at the joints. This happens again and again.

Muscles, joints, and bones are like a team. They all work together to help you move.

Your bones, joints, and muscles get you where you want to go. Some foods can make your bones and muscles grow well. Running and jumping can help make bones and muscles strong.

REVIEW

1. What do your bones do for you?

2. What moves your bones?

3. How can you keep your bones and muscles strong?

4. **Infer** What muscles do you use to play ball?

5. **Think and Write** Explain how your leg bends.

Topic 3
THE HUMAN BODY

Why it matters

We need to take care of our skin.

Science Words

skin covers your body and helps you touch and feel

germs tiny living things that can make you sick

The Outside of You

What covers the outsides of the things here? Which outsides are soft? Which outsides are hard? What else could you say about the outsides of these things?

EXPLORE

What covers the outside of you?

What can you find out about skin?

In this activity you will observe your skin up close.

What you need

- hand lens
- pencil
- *Science Journal*

What to do

1. Trace your hand in the *Science Journal*.

2. **Observe** Look at the back of your hand with a hand lens. Draw what you see.

3. Press your hand hard with your other hand. What do you feel?

What did you find out?

1. **Compare** Did all parts of your hand look the same? Explain.

2. **Identify** What grows out of your skin?

3. **Infer** What did you feel in step 3?

What is skin?

The Explore Activity shows how **skin** looks up close. Skin covers your body and helps you touch and feel. It is smooth and soft. It is tough, too. You can press skin and pinch it. You can wet it and tickle it.

If you cut your skin, it hurts. A cut can let in **germs.** Germs are tiny living things that can make you sick. They are too small to be seen. Your skin helps keep germs out.

As your bones grow, your skin grows, too.

What's in skin? READING LINK

Skin is thin, but it does a lot. Your skin helps you touch and feel the world around you.

Can you find the hair? It starts down in the skin and then grows out of it. Something else comes out of skin. It is sweat. Sweat is mostly water. Sweat helps you stay cool.

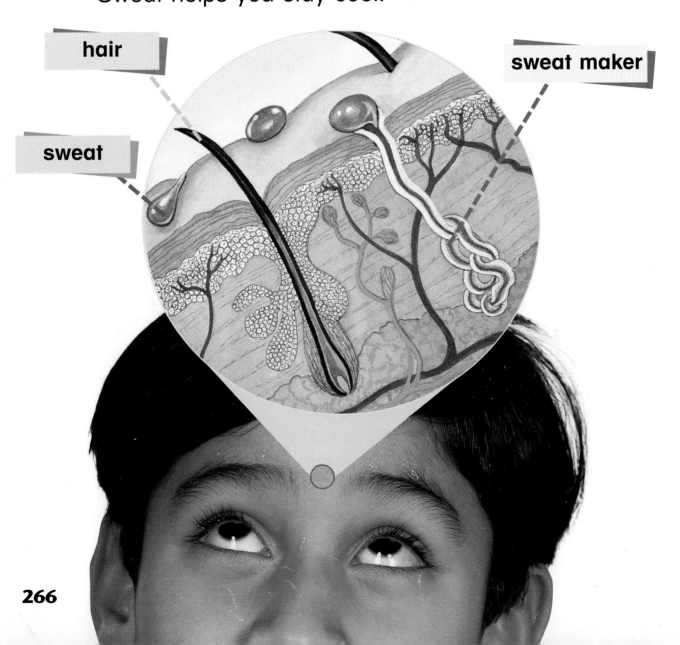

hair

sweat

sweat maker

Your skin does many jobs. It is important to take care of your skin. Too much sun can harm your skin. How does this child take care of her skin?

1. What does your skin do for you?

2. What comes out of skin?

3. What does your skin help you feel?

4. **Communicate** Make a list of what you can do to take care of your skin.

5. **Think and Write** Why do you sweat when you run and play hard?

SCIENCE MAGAZINE

WHAT'S INSIDE?

Can you see your insides? No, but a machine can. It takes X-ray pictures!

A scientist named Marie Curie helped make X-rays. X-rays pass through your skin and muscles, but not through bones. Your bones look like shadows on an X ray.

Dentists take X rays, too. A cavity looks like a big hole!

Doctors take X rays of broken bones. The X rays show where bones are broken. Then doctors fix the bones so they heal!

Doctors may also take pictures with an imager. It uses a special magnet to make pictures of body parts.

DISCUSS

1. What machines can take pictures of your insides?
2. Why might doctors need to see what's inside you?

269

Use Science Words

germ

joints

muscle

skeleton

skin

1. A body frame made up of bones is a ___?___. page 256

2. Bones meet at the ___?___. page 259

3. The part of your body that can move a bone by pulling on it is a ___?___. page 258

4. Your body is covered by ___?___. page 264

5. A tiny living thing that can make you sick is called a ___?___. page 265

Use Science Ideas

Match each word to its picture. pages 258–259, 266

hair   joint   muscle

6.   7.   8.

9. Describe how you have grown this year. pages 244–245

10. **Infer** Last year's clothes feel tight. Why? page 244

PROBLEMS and PUZZLES

See Through Put your fingers over a lit flashlight. What do you see inside your fingers? Can you see the bones of your hand? Draw what you see.

Use Science Words

germs	height	joint	skeleton	skin

1. You can use numbers to measure your __?__.

2. All your bones make up your __?__.

3. The place where your bones meet is a __?__.

4. The thing that helps you feel is your __?__.

5. Your skin helps keep out __?__.

Use Science Ideas

6. How can you tell that you have grown?

7. What makes your bones move?

8. What keeps your muscles strong?

9. How are an egg shell and your skin alike?

10. **Use Numbers** Copy the chart on the right. Put the numbers 112, 50, and 165 where they belong.

Amy's Height in cm	
At Birth	
In First Grade	
Grown Up	

Write in Your Journal

What do you see?
Write about it.

PROBLEMS and PUZZLES

Move It!

Run, dance, skip, walk or touch your toes.
Which parts of your body have to move?
Which parts have to bend, twist, or turn?
Make a list.

What Moves?

Pick a game or sport that you like to play.
Try to find out which body parts you move
when you play it.
Draw a picture and tell the class which
parts move.

REFERENCE SECTION

PICTURE BUILDERS

Building a Pond

What animals do you see at the pond? What plants do you see?

BASE

Look on the next page. Lift up all the clear sheets (1, 2, 3). These are the overlays. The page on the bottom is the base. Look at the base. **What part of the pond do you see? What plants and animals live there?**

OVERLAY 1

Drop overlay 1 down onto the base. **What part was added to the pond? What animals live there?**

OVERLAY 2

Drop overlay 2 down. **What do you see now?**

OVERLAY 3

Drop overlay 3 down. **What do you see now?**

SUM UP

What are the parts of the pond? What animals live at each part?

BASE: Start with a pond.

PICTURE BUILDERS
Activities

1 Act Out a Picture

You need: chalk

Draw the shape of a pond as it looks in this picture. Draw it on the playground floor. Make it really big. Ten friends go to different parts of the pond. Each friend says out loud what animal he or she may be.

2 Write About It

Pick an animal from the pond. Write about it. Tell what it does at the pond.

REFERENCE SECTION

HANDBOOK

Stay Safe

We need to stay safe.
Here are some safety tips.

Classroom Safety Tips

- Read all steps a few times before you start.
- Listen to the teacher.
- When you see this ▨, it means for you to be careful.
- 🥽 Wear goggles or gloves when told.
- Wear old clothes.
- Be careful with glass and sharp objects.
- Never taste or smell things unless your teacher tells you to.
- Tell about spills right away.
- Tell about accidents right away.
- Keep your work place neat.
- Clean up when you are done.

Outside Safety Tips

- Listen to the teacher.
- Stay with your group.
- Never taste or smell things unless your teacher tells you to.
- Don't touch plants or animals unless your teacher tells you to.
- Put living things back where you found them.
- Tell about accidents right away.

Save and Recycle

We should not waste things.

Use no more than
you need.

Don't leave the water on.

Use things more than
one time.

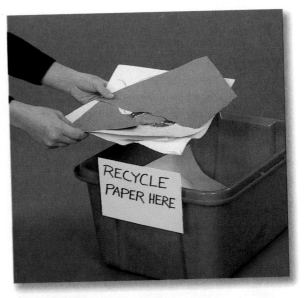

RECYCLE
PAPER HERE

Recycle as much as
you can.

Clean Up

We need to clean up work places.

Let an adult clean up broken glass.

Pour water into a sink, not into a trash can.

Don't get paint or food on you.

Put food in plastic bags. This keeps bugs away.

Care of Plants

Here are ways to care for plants.

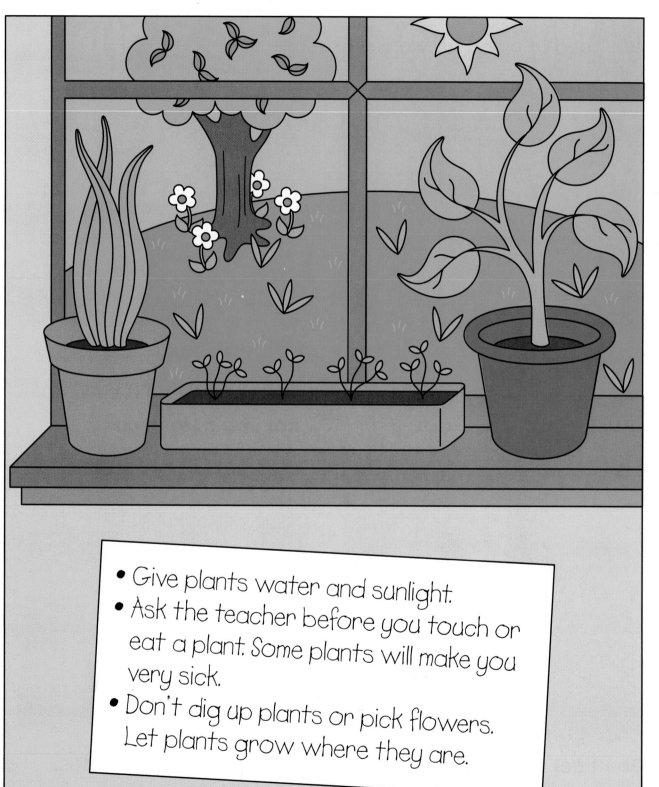

- Give plants water and sunlight.
- Ask the teacher before you touch or eat a plant. Some plants will make you very sick.
- Don't dig up plants or pick flowers. Let plants grow where they are.

Care of Animals

Here are ways to care for animals.

- Give animals food and water. Give them a safe place to live, too.
- Be kind to animals. Handle them with care.
- Look at wild animals. Don't touch them. They may bite, sting, or scratch.
- Leave the places where animals live alone.

How to Measure

You can use many things to measure.

This string is about 8 paper clips long.

This string is about 3 pencils long.

This string is about 2 hands long.

Try It

1. Measure some string. Tell how you did it.
2. Can you measure string with these paper clips?
   Why or why not?

Units of Measurement

People don't measure with paper clips.

They use centimeters (cm) or meters (m).

These are called units of measurement.

The crayon is about 8 centimeters long.

We write this as 8 cm.

The bug is about 4 centimeters long.

We write this as 4 cm.

Try It

1. How long is the pencil?

2. How long is the worm?

Use a Ruler

```
|  |  |  |  |  |  |  |  |  |  |  |  |  |  |  |
0  1  2  3  4  5  6  7  8  9  10 11 12 13 14
centimeters
```

You can use a ruler to measure this leaf.
Line up the end of the leaf with the 0 on
the ruler.
The leaf is about I I centimeters or I I cm.

Try It

Find each object.
Estimate how long.
Use a ruler to measure.

	Estimate	Measure
?	about _?_ cm	about _?_ cm
?	about _?_ cm	about _?_ cm
?	about _?_ cm	about _?_ cm

Use a Meterstick

A meterstick is 1 meter or
100 centimeters long.
This dog is about 1 meter tall.

A meterstick is used to measure
long or tall objects.
Use a meterstick just like a ruler.

Try It

Estimate how high or long.
Use a meterstick to measure.

	Estimate	Measure
	about _?_ m	about _?_ m
	about _?_ m	about _?_ m
	about _?_ m	about _?_ m

Use a Thermometer

A thermometer measures temperature.

It gets warmer. The liquid in a thermometer moves up.

It gets cooler. The liquid in a thermometer moves down.

Which thermometer shows a warmer temperature? How can you tell?

A thermometer has marks with numbers.
This thermometer shows degrees Fahrenheit and degrees Celsius.
Each mark means 2 degrees.

Read this thermometer in degrees Celsius.
Find the number just below where the liquid ends.
The number is 20.
Count on 2 degrees for each mark after 20 as: 22, 24, 26.
The thermometer shows 26 degrees Celsius, or 26°C.

Try It

What temperatures are shown on page R12?

Use a Measuring Cup

Volume is the amount of space something takes up.
Use a measuring cup to find volume.
There are 200 milliliters (200 mL) of water in this cup.

— 250 mL

— 175 mL

—100 mL

— 25 mL

Try It

1. Get 3 different small containers.

2. Which holds the most? Which holds the least?

3. Fill each container with water. Pour the water into the measuring cup. Find the volumes.

Use a Balance

A balance compares mass.

Before you compare mass, make sure the arrow points to the line.

Place an object on each pan.
The object that has more mass will make that side of the balance go down.
The object that has less mass will make that side of the balance go up.

Try It

1. Place 2 objects on a balance.
2. Which has more mass?

Try It

1. Place 3 objects in order from least mass to most mass.
2. Use the balance to check.

Use a Clock

A clock measures time.
Each mark means 1 minute.
There are 5 minutes between
each number.
There are 60 minutes in 1 hour.

hour hand   minute hand

30 minutes after 1 o'clock
1:30

5 minutes after 9 o'clock
9:05

Try It

How long do you think it takes to
write your name 5 times? Have a
friend time you.

R16

Use a Hand Lens

A hand lens makes objects seem larger.

To use a hand lens:

Step 1: Move the lens away from the object.
Stop when the object looks fuzzy.

Step 2: Move the lens a little closer
to the object.
Stop when the object looks clear.

Step 1   Step 2

Try It

1. Observe each animal.
   Use a hand lens.

spider

fly

2. How many legs do you see on the spider?

3. What else can you see?

Use a Computer

A computer is a tool that can get information.

You can use the Internet. The Internet links your computer to ones far away.

You can also use CD-ROMs. They have a lot of information. You can fit many books on one CD-ROM!

Try It

1. Use the Internet. Find out how warm it is where you live.
2. Use the Internet. Find out how warm it is in a different place.

Record and Compare

You can write information in a chart.
You can use this information.

This chart shows information about
leaves that some children found.

Name	smooth-edged leaves	saw-toothed leaves
Mark	4	6
Kim	5	5
Bonnie	3	7

Try It

1. How many children found leaves?
2. What kinds of leaves did the children find?
3. How many leaves did Bonnie find?

Observe Parts

The parts of a machine work together.

Try It

Name the parts of each machine.

How Parts Work Together

A machine needs all its parts to work.

What part is missing?

GLOSSARY

B

branches the part that holds the leaves of a tree *(page 8)*

> Monkeys swing on the branches of a tree.

C

classify to put things into groups *(page 198)*

> Tim will classify his marbles into big and small.

clouds small drops of water that float in the sky *(page 67)*

> Gray clouds come before the rain.

communicate to talk, write, or draw *(page 150)*

> Keenan communicates well with his sister.

constellation picture in the night sky made by stars *(page 90)*

> The Big Dipper is a constellation in the sky.

E

evergreen a plant that stays green all year *(page 26)*

An evergreen tree stays green even in winter.

F

food chain shows you what animals eat *(page 228)*

Plants are part of many food chains.

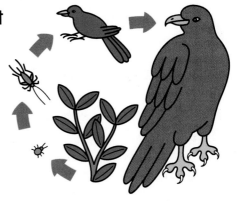

force what makes an object move *(page 157)*

A pushing force moves the sofa.

freeze when a liquid changes to a solid *(page 210)*

You freeze water to make ice cubes.

G

gases something that has no size or shape of its own *(page 131)*

Air is made up of many gases.

R23

germs tiny living things that can make you sick *(page 265)*

> **Germs are too small to see.**

H

habitat where animals and plants live and grow *(page 197)*

> **A cave is a good habitat for a bear.**

heat to make warmer or hotter *(page 53)*

> **You can heat water on a stove.**

I

infer to use what you know to figure something out *(page 54)*

> **You can infer from the footprints where the dog went.**

J

joint a place where bones meet *(page 259)*

> **Your elbow bends at the joint.**

L

leaves the part of a tree that makes food *(page 4)*

> The leaves **grow on the branches of trees.**

living thing something that grows and changes *(page 12)*

> Living things **need food, air, and water.**

liquid something that has no shape of its own *(page 124)*

> You can fill a jar with **liquid.**

M

mass how much matter is in an object *(page 109)*

> **The object with more mass is heavier.**

less mass

more mass

matter the stuff all things are made of *(page 108)*

> **Different things are made of matter.**

measure to find out the size or amount of something *(page 102)*

> **You can use a ruler to measure this book.**

melt to change from a solid to a liquid *(page 136)*

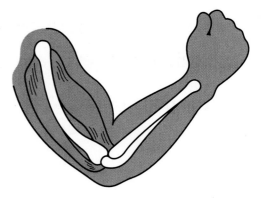

> **The flame melts the candle.**

Moon a large ball of rock that moves around Earth *(page 82)*

> **You see the Moon at night.**

move to go from one place to another *(page 148)*

> **The dog uses its legs to move.**

muscle a body part that can move a bone by pulling on it *(page 258)*

> **You can feel the muscle in your arm.**

N

natural resource something we use that comes from Earth *(page 36)*

We must take care of our natural resources.

needs what all living things must have to stay alive *(page 184)*

The baby bird needs shelter and food.

nonliving things things that do not grow, breathe, or need food *(page 204)*

A rock, flashlight, and bucket are examples of nonliving things.

O

observe to use your senses to learn something *(page 6)*

The boy observes the rock.

P

part a piece of an object *(page 162)*

Cut an orange into many parts.

pond water with land all around *(page 196)*

Many plants and animals live in or near a pond.

position where an object is *(page 148)*

The truck is in a different position from the car.

properties how a thing looks, feels, smells, tastes, or sounds *(page 100)*

A rock has many properties.

pull to move an object closer *(page 157)*

A girl pulls the leash on her dog.

push to move an object away *(page 156)*

The baby pushes the food away.

R

roots the part of a tree that takes in water *(page 5)*

> **The roots of a tree are under the ground.**

S

seasons spring, summer, fall, and winter *(page 72)*

> **A year has four seasons.**

seed the part of a plant that has a new plant inside *(page 18)*

> **An apple has seeds.**

seedling a small new plant *(page 18)*

> **Plant a seedling.**

shadow it is made when something is in the way of light *(page 60)*

> **The girl's shadow jumps when she jumps.**

shelter something that covers or protects *(page 40)*

> **Paul and Maria use a tent for shelter.**

skeleton a body frame made up of bones *(page 256)*

> **The skeleton holds up the body.**

skin the body part that covers your body and keeps your insides in *(page 264)*

> **You can pinch your skin.**

solid something with a shape and a size *(page 118)*

> **Toy blocks are solid.**

stars objects that make their own light *(page 88)*

> **Stars are far away in the sky.**

survive to stay alive *(page 233)*

Some animals survive by hiding.

T

tadpole a young frog *(page 220)*

Tadpoles grow up to be frogs.

temperature how warm or cool something is *(page 52)*

The temperature is high in the summer.

trunk the part that is the stem of a tree *(page 8)*

The trunk is the widest part of a tree.

W

whole all the parts together *(page 162)*

You can buy a watermelon whole or in slices.

CREDITS

Design & Production: Kirchoff/Wohlberg, Inc.

Maps: Geosystems.

Transvision: David Mager (photography); Michael Maydak (illustration).

Illustrations:

Neesa Becker: pp. 243, 270; Ka Botzis: pp. 204–205, 228; Elizabeth Callen: pp. 4, 5, 8, 12, 13, 14, 15, 90, 153, 159, 170, 171, 174, 190, 192; Barbara Cousins: pp. 257, 265, 270; Mike DiGiorgio: 188–189; Jeff Fagan: 44-45; Kristen Goeters: pp. 30, 46, 111, 114, 142, 143, 144, 191, 199, 200–201, 213, 216, 246, 252, 272; Virge Kask: pp. 4–5, 15, 30, 37, 46, 47, 232, 233, 235, 238; Tom Leonard: pp. 226–227, 240; Claude Martinot: pp. 6, 34, 35, 48, 54, 78, 146, 166, 185, 235, 238; Sharron O'Neil: pp. 196–197, 210–211, 212, 223, 258–259, 266; Monika Popowitz: pp. 43, 108–109; Rob Schuster: pp. 82–83, 84, 94, 96, 138; Sarah Snow: pp. 52–53; Craig Spearing: p. 91; Matt Straub: pp. 56, 60; Ted Williams: pp. 162, 163. Handbook: Batelman: pp. R10, R11, R14, R19; Rita Lascaro: pp. R2, R3, R6, R7; Rob Schuster: pp. R12, R13, R20, R21; Ted Williams: pp. R8, R9, R16–R18. Glossary: Batelman: pp. R22, R25, R28, R30, R31; Eileen Hine: pp. R22, R24, R26, R27, R28, R29, R31; Rita Lascaro: pp. R22, R23, R24, R25, R26, R27, R28, R29, R30, R31.

Photography Credits:

Contents: iii: Ron Thomas/FPG. iv: Telegraph Colour Library/FPG. v: VCG/FPG. vi: Terry Qing/FPG. vii: Gary W. Carter/Visuals Unlimited. viii: Roy Morsch/The Stock Market.

National Geographic Invitation to Science: S2: Christina M. Allen. S3: t, Christina M. Allen; m, Gregory G. Dimijian/Photo Researchers, Inc.; b, Christina M. Allen.

Be a Scientist: S4: James Shnepf/Liaison International. S5: MMSD. S6: Charles Gupton/Tony Stone Images. S7: Jon Muresan/MMD. S8: Jon Muresan/MMD. S9: Steven Peters/Tony Stone Images. S10: David Joel/Tony Stone Images. S11: Bruce Ayres/Tony Stone Images. S12: Richard Hutchings/Photo Researchers, Inc. S13: Superstock. S14: Michael Newman/PhotoEdit. S15: t, Superstock; b, Telegraph Colour Library/FPG. S16: t, B. Daemmrich/The Image Works; b, D. Young-Wolff/PhotoEdit. S17: Image Bank. S18: l, Hunter Freeman/ Liaison International; r, Richard Hutchings/PhotoEdit. S19: l, Superstock; r, Tony Freeman/PhotoEdit. S20: Richard Hutchings/PhotoEdit.

Unit 1: 1: George Ranalli/Photo Researchers, Inc. 2: Debra P Hershkowitz/Bruce Coleman, Inc. 3: David Mager. 5: Gary Braasch/AllStock/PNI. 6: F. Stuart Westmorland/Photo Researchers, Inc. 7: McGraw-Hill School Division. 8: Herbert Kehrer/Okapia/ Photo Researchers, Inc. 9: Sharon Cummings/Dembinsky Photo Assoc. 10: l. Wendell Metzen/Bruce Coleman, Inc.; r. Lance Nelson/The Stock Market. 11: David Mager. 12: Jane Burton/Bruce Coleman, Inc. 13: l. Bill Bachmann/Photo Researchers, Inc.; r. Francois Gohier/Photo Researchers, Inc. 14: l. Robert Planck/Dembinsky Photo Assoc.; r. Brian Yarvin/Photo Researchers, Inc. 16: Joseph Mettis/Photo Researchers, Inc.17: David Mager. 18: l. David Mager; inset, Jerome Wezler/Photo Researchers, Inc. 18–19: Keith Campagna. 19: PhotoDisc. 20: l. Robert P. Carr/Bruce Coleman, Inc.; t. Michael P. Gadomski/Photo Researchers, Inc.; b. John Markham/Bruce Coleman, Inc. 21: t. David Mager; b.l. Jerome Wexler/Photo Researchers, Inc.; b. Erwin & Peggy Bauer/Bruce Coleman, Inc. 22: l.&r. Hermann Eisenbeiss/Photo Researchers, Inc. 23: McGraw-Hill School Division. 24: l.&r. Laura Riley/Bruce Coleman, Inc. 25: l.&r. Laura Riley/Bruce Coleman, Inc. 26: l. Joe Bator/The Stock Market; inset, Noble Proctor/Photo Researchers, Inc. 27: Bonnie Rauch/Photo Researchers, Inc. 28: l. Lori Adamski Peek/Tony Stone Images; r. Carolina Biological Supply/Phototake. 29: t. Albinger Mauritius GMBH/Phototake; b. Bob Daemmrich/Stock, Boston/PNI. 31: Jim Cummins/FPG. 32: David Mager. 33: David Mager. 34: PhotoDisc.; m. l.: Antonio M. Rosario/Image Bank. 35: l. Debra Hershkowitz/Bruce Coleman, Inc.; r. Chuck Savage/The Stock Market. 36: Joe Feingersh/The Stock Market. 37: David Mager. 38: Ron Austing/Photo Researchers, Inc. 39: David Mager. 40: t. Karen McGougan/ Bruce Coleman, Inc.; l. Jim W. Grace/Photo Researchers, Inc.; r. Tom & Pat Leesen/Photo Researchers, Inc. 41: l. Alan D. Carey/Photo Researchers, Inc.; r. Mark Boulton/Photo Researchers, Inc.; b. Gregory K. Scott/Photo Researchers, Inc. 42: inset, Gregory K. Scott/Photo Researchers, Inc.; b.r. Stephen J. Krasemann/ Photo Researchers, Inc. 46: Stephen J. Krasemann/Photo Researchers, Inc.

Unit 2: 49: Bill Ross/Westlight. 50: Lawrence Migdale/Photo Researchers, Inc. 51: David Mager. 52: Myrleen Ferguson/PhotoEdit. 54: l. PhotoDisc; r. RB Studio/The Stock Market. 55: David Mager. 56: t. Richard Hutchings/PhotoEdit; b. Michael Newman/PhotoEdit. 57: Barbara Gerlach/Dembinsky Photo Assoc. 58: David Mager. 59: David Mager. 60: Barry Hennings/Photo Researchers, Inc. 61: Debra P. Hershkowitz. 62: t. Nornert Schafer/The Stock Market; b. Keith Gunnar/Bruce Coleman, Inc./PNI. 63: Sandy King/The Image Bank. 64: David Young-Wolff/PhotoEdit. 65: David Mager. 66: t.l. Francis/Donna Caldwell/Visuals Unlimited; t.r. C/B Productions/The Stock Market; b.l. David Madison/Bruce Coleman, Inc.; m.r.&b.r. PhotoDisc. 67: t. Karen McGougan/Bruce Coleman, Inc; b. A & J Verkaik/The Stock Market. 68: t. Tom McCarthy/Photo Researchers, Inc.; m. John H. Hoffman/Bruce Coleman, Inc.; b. Jeff Greenberg/PhotoEdit. 69: David Mager. 70: David Mager. 71: David Mager. 72: t.l.&b.l. David Mager; t.r. Don Hebert/FPG; b.l. Larry Lefever/Grant Heilman. 73: t.l.&b.r. David Mager; b.l. Mark E. Gibson/Dembinsky Photo Assoc.; t.r. Richard Hutchings/Photo Researchers, Inc. 74: l. Greg Probst/Tony Stone Images; r. Ron Thomas/FPG. 75: Tom Bean/The Stock

Market. 79: Zefa/Stock Imagery, Inc. 81: David Mager. 82–83: NASA. 85: David Mager. 86: Jerry Schad/Photo Researchers, Inc. 87: David Mager. 88: Jerry Schad/Science/Photo Researchers, Inc. 89: NASA. 90: John R. Foster/Photo Researchers, Inc.92–93: NASA. 93: t., m., b. Corbis/Bettmann.

Unit 3: p. 97: inset, ZEFA/Stock Imagery, bkgrd, ZEFA/Stock Imagery. 98: David Mager. 99: David Mager. 100: l. Elizabeth Hathon/The Stock Market; r. Jeff Greenberg/Photo Researchers, Inc.; b.l. David Mager. 101: t.l. David Mager; l. Paul Barton/The Stock Market; r. Ken Chemus/FPG. 102: David Mager. 103: David Mager. 104: David Mager. 105: Jane Burton/Bruce Coleman, Inc. 106: David Mager. 107: David Mager. 109: Painting by Larry Foster. 110: David Mager. 111: David Mager. 112: t. Cheryl Hogue/Visuals Unlimited; inset t. Todd Gipstein/National Geographic Image Collection; b. Raymond Gehman. 113: t.l. A. Farnsworth/The Image Works; t.r. Coco McCoy/Rainbow; m. Lynn M. Stone; b. Spencer Swagner/Tom Stack & Associates. p. 115: David Noble/FPG. 116: l. Michael S. Yamashita/Corbis; r. Louie Psihoyos/The Stock Market. 117: David Mager. 118: David Mager. 119: David Mager. 120: David Mager. 121: David Mager. 122: David Mager. 123: David Mager. 124–125: David Mager. 126: David Mager. 127: Jim Cummins/FPG. 128: Collins/ Monkmeyer 129: David Mager. 130–131: David Mager. 132: l. Kagan/Monkmeyer; r. Jean Miele/Monkmeyer. 133: l. David Mager; r. Ariel Skelley/The Stock Market. 134: Jose L. Pelaez/The Stock Market. 135: David Mager. 136: l. Harry Hartman/ Bruce Coleman, Inc.; r. Michael Keller/FPG. 137: Lew Merrim/Monkmeyer. 139: t.r. M.J. Manuel/Photo Researchers, Inc.; b. Craig Lovell/Corbis. 140: Binney & Smith Properties; PhotoDisc. 141: Binney & Smith Properties; PhotoDisc. 144: David Mager.

Unit 4: p. 145: bkgrd, Will Ryan/The Stock Market; inset, Rudi VonBriel/Photo Edit. 146: David Mager. 147: David Mager. 148: David Mager. 149: David Mager. 150: l. Tom McHugh/Photo Researchers, Inc.; r. Mark J. Thomas/Dembinsky Photo Assoc. 151: David Mager. 152: David Mager. 154: David Madison/Bruce Coleman, Inc. 155: David Mager. 156: David Mager. 157: David Mager. 158: t. David Mager.; b. T.J. Florian/Rainbow. 159: Jeff Greenberg/Photo Researchers, Inc. 160: David Mager. 161: David Mager. 164: t. David Mager; b. Michael Newman/PhotoEdit. 165: George Shelley/The Stock Market. 166: Peter Beck/The Stock Market. 167: David Mager. 168: David Mager. 169: David Mager. 171: Stephanie Rausser/FPG. 172: Peter Cade/Tony Stone Images.173: t.l. Philip John Bailey/Stock, Boston/PNI; m.l. Pete Winkel/Stock South/PNI; t.r. Tony Freeman/PhotoEdit; b.r. Tony Stone Images. 175: inset, Rudi VonBriel/Photo Edit; bkgrd, Fritz Polking/Photo Researchers, Inc.; Manoj Shah/Tony Stone Images. 176: Mark Gamba/The Stock Market. 177: David Mager. 180: t.r. Maslowski/Photo Researchers, Inc.; m.r. Carol Hughes/Bruce Coleman, Inc.; l. Y. Arthus-Bertrand/ Peter Arnold, Inc.; b. Stephen Frink/The Stock Market. 181: Foto Sorrel/Peter Arnold, Inc. 182: Bob & Clara Calhoun/Bruce Coleman, Inc. 183: David Mager. 184: t.l. Kim Taylor/Bruce Coleman, Inc.; t.r. Zefa Germany/The Stock Market; b. Larry Lipsky/ Bruce Coleman, Inc. 185: t. Rob Planck/Bruce Coleman, Inc.; b. J.C. Carton/Bruce Coleman, Inc. 186: David Madison/Bruce Coleman, Inc. 187: Renee Lynn/Photo Researchers, Inc. 189: Joe McDonald/Visuals Unlimited.

Unit 5: p. 193: S.R. Maglione/Photo Researchers Inc. 194: Ellan Young/Photo Researchers, Inc. 195: David Mager. 198: t.r. J. C. Carton/Bruce Coleman, Inc.; b.r. Jim Zipp/Photo Researchers, Inc.; t.l. John Shaw/Bruce Coleman, Inc.; b.l. Stan Osolinski/The Stock Market. 199: David Mager. 200: t. Edward R. Degginger/ Dembinsky Photo Assoc.; b. Ken Wilson/Papilio/ Corbis. 201: Wayne Lankinen/Bruce Coleman, Inc. 202: Adam Jones/Dembinsky Photo Assoc. 203: David Mager. 205: Rick Poley/Visuals Unlimited. 206: inset, Dwight R. Kuhn/Dwight Kuhn; b. John Hyde/Bruce Coleman, Inc. 207: David Mager. 208: Pat Anderson/Visuals Unlimited. 209: David Mager. 213: Adam Jones/ Dembinsky Photo Assoc. 214: b.l. Raymond K. Gehman; t. Chris Johns/National Geographic. 215: t. Tony Freeman/PhotoEdit; b. Jeff Greenberg/The Image Works. p. 217: bkgrd, Eunice Harris/Photo Researchers; inset, Larry West/FPG. 218: Marianne Dube. 219: David Mager. 220: b. Dwight R. Kuhn/Dwight Kuhn; t. John Shaw/Bruce Coleman, Inc.; 221: t. Dwight R. Kuhn/Dwight Kuhn; b. Joe McDonald/Bruce Coleman, Inc. 222: S. Nielsen/Bruce Coleman, Inc. 224: Jane Burton/Bruce Coleman, Inc. 229: Gary Meszaros/Bruce Coleman, Inc. 230: Skip Moody/Dembinsky Photo Assoc. 231: David Mager. 232: Joe McDonald/Bruce Coleman, Inc. 233: Larry Mishkar/Dembinsky Photo Assoc. 234: b. Joe McDonald/Visuals Unlimited; t. Skip Moody/Dembinsky Photo Assoc. 235: Adam Jones/Dembinsky Photo Assoc. 236: inset, Brian Stablyk/Tony Stone Images; bkgrd. David Muench/Tony Stone Images. 237: inset, b. Daniel J. Cox/Tony Stone Images; bkgrd. Frans Lanting/Tony Stone Images; inset, t. K. Schafer & M. Hill/Tony Stone Images. 239: Jim Battles/Dembinsky Photo Assoc.

Unit 6: 241: inset, David Mager; bkgrd, Photo Disc. 242: Chuck Savage/The Stock Market. 243: David Mager. 244: inset, David Mager; l. Myrleen Ferguson/PhotoEdit. 245: r. Charles Gupton/The Stock Market; l. David Mager. 246: Volkmar Wentzel. 247: David Mager. 248: t.l. Paul Barton/The Stock Market; t.r. Eastcott/Momatiuk Woodfin Camp & Assoc.; b. Ronnie Kaufman/The Stock Market. 249: b.r. J. Pinderhughes/The Stock Market; l. Myrleen Cate/PhotoEdit. 250–251: Robert Pearcy/Animals Animals; Brian Kenney. p. 253: Arthur Tilley/FPG. 254: r. David Young-Wolff/PhotoEdit; l. Mark M. Lawrence/The Stock Market. 255: David Mager. 256: t. Craig Hammell/The Stock Market; b. Paul Steel/The Stock Market. 258–259: David Mager. 260: Kim Barth/The Chronicle Telegram. 261: r. David Mager; l. Tony Freeman/PhotoEdit. 262: David Mager. 263: David Mager. 264: David Mager. 265: David Mager. 266: David Mager. 267: Jim Whitmer/FPG. 268: PhotoDisc. 269: m. Bachmann/Photo Researchers, Inc.; b. Brownie Harris/The Stock Market; t. Gerald & Buff Corsi/Visuals Unlimited. 271: Dennis Potokar/Photo Researchers, Inc.

Handbook: David Mager: pp. R4, R5, R15